BCWALKER

D1438206

MAP READING AND INTERPRETATION

MAP READING AND INTERPRETATION

New Edition with Metric Examples

P. SPEAK, M.A., F.R.G.S.
Head of School of Geography

A. H. C. CARTER, B.Sc.
Senior Lecturer in Geography
Cambridgeshire College of Arts and Technology

LONGMAN

ACKNOWLEDGEMENTS

LONGMAN GROUP LIMITED
London

Associated companies, branches and representatives throughout the world

© P. Speak and A. H. C. Carter 1964; 1970
This edition © Longman Group Ltd 1970

All rights reserved. No part of this publication may be reproduced, stored in a retrieval system or transmitted in any form or by any means—electronic, mechanical, photocopying, or otherwise—without the prior permission of the copyright owner

First published 1964
Second Edition with metric examples 1970

ISBN 0 582 31010 5

We are pleased to acknowledge gratefully our thanks to Mr D. R. Staveley, of Wymondham College, Norfolk, and Mr W. Islip, of the Cambridgeshire College of Arts and Technology for helpful advice in the preparation of the text, to Mr R. Lindsay for specially taking Plate VIII, to Mrs E. Butler for typing the manuscript and to Professor F. J. Monkhouse, who advised on the editing of the typescript and offered many valuable suggestions on the text and diagrams, which we were pleased to incorporate.

Ordnance Survey map extracts, conventional signs and the explanation of the National Grid together with the map extract on the front cover are reproduced by permission of the Controller of Her Majesty's Stationery Office and figures 10b, 10c, 10d, 24, 25, 26a, 26b, 27, 28, 29, 30, 38, and 40, are based by permission on maps published by the Ordnance Survey. We are also indebted to the Director-General of the Ordnance Survey for much detailed information, generously given.

Dr J. K. St Joseph, Curator of the Department of Aerial Photography, University of Cambridge, and the Librarian of Aerofilms, kindly selected many photographs for our inspection. Acknowledgement of copyright is given below. Plates 1, 5, 7 are by J. K. St. Joseph, Crown Copyright Reserved; Plate 2, Crown Copyright Reserved; Plate 4, J. K. St. Joseph, University of Cambridge; Plates 3, 6, and 9, Aerofilms; Plate 8, R. Lindsay. The photograph used on the cover is Crown Copyright Reserved.

Our sincere thanks go to Mr E. W. Parker lately of Longmans, who gave us every assistance and encouragement in the preparation of the book at all stages. The maps and diagrams were drawn by A. W. Gatrell & Co. Ltd.

Printed in Great Britain by
Lowe & Brydone (Printers) Ltd., London, N.W.10

FOREWORD

Our aims in offering this book are threefold: firstly, to cover the essential mapwork for the compulsory map interpretation questions set in the Ordinary level papers of the General Certificate of Education; secondly, to bridge the gap between Ordinary level and more advanced work, particularly for those students taking the Ordinary Alternative paper in Geography at Advanced level, and, thirdly, to provide a set of Ordnance Survey map extracts which illustrate the great variety of landscapes found within the British Isles. The work is presented as a systematic text with questions at the end of Part One and in Part Three, and is intended for use in the upper forms of schools and in the intensive courses given in Technical Colleges. We assume that the reader will have completed simple map reading exercises, such as in the recognition of O.S. symbols and the use of the National Grid, and have some elementary knowledge of the principles of physical geography.

Part One deals with map reading and describes various techniques of map measurement of scale, direction, area and relief. The aim is to provide methods that are simple and quick in the examination room without any loss of accuracy or detail. Part Two sets out a logical approach to map interpretation, dealing in turn, with the recognition of land forms, the identification of rocks, settlement, communications, and land use. The method is then applied in turn to each of the map extracts in Part Three and a detailed analysis of each sheet is given.

All the plates are complementary to the maps and provide the opportunity for additional questions on photograph interpretation. Wherever suitable as illustrations, block diagrams have been used to help in the realization of the three-dimensional form portrayed in the map. The O.S. map fragments illustrate all the material in Parts One and Two, and each map serves to show one major aspect of map interpretation. Equal weight has been given to the 1 : 25,000 and the one-inch maps; to give more variety and added interest in map scale and style, a six inch O.S. extract has been included and the Lake District one inch map is in the style of the latest hill-shaded Tourist edition. Those sketchmaps based on Ordnance Survey maps have been drawn carefully in order to preserve the reality of the originals and have not been over-simplified.

The questions and specimen examination papers following each map analysis have been framed according to the standards of recent examination papers. The techniques and exercises have been tried ' on the dog ' for many years and we hope, as teachers and examiners, that this book will go some way to meet the rising standards of the examination paper.

P. Speak.
A. H. C. Carter.
Cambridgeshire College of Arts and Technology.
1963.

Note to Second Impression: We are grateful to several correspondents for suggestions which have been incorporated in this printing. The Ordnance Survey maps in Part Three have been printed as far as possible in the standard colours of the official maps within the economic limits of lithographic reproduction. On some maps the National Grid lines are in green instead of the conventional black or grey; urban areas and land-use symbols are shown in a warmer grey than that of the official series. These slight differences should not confuse the student in any way when presented with map extracts in the examination room.

FOREWORD TO THE NEW EDITION WITH METRIC EXAMPLES

The 1970s should see the gradual introduction of metrication to all kinds of measurement in the United Kingdom. Some weights and measures are already in metric form, the decimalisation of coinage will be completed in February, 1971, and eventually all official map scales will be published in metric editions. For the Ordnance Survey this means an immense task of map revision as it involves the replacement of the one inch and six inch scales by metric alternatives and the alteration of foot heights to metres. No decision has yet been made by the Ordnance Survey about the details of metrication of the one inch and smaller scale maps but map extracts at 1 : 50,000 and 1 : 25,000 suitable for examination purposes are being published by them. We have therefore included in this reprint two examples of metric maps, the 1 : 50,000 of the area around Dorking and the 1 : 25,000 of part of the east Devon coast near Exmouth, together with appropriate map analysis and questions and an enlargement of section on scales, direction and areas. It is most likely that by 1975 sufficient extracts will be available for examination boards to set metric examples in their Geography papers and this will obviously affect those pupils entering secondary education in 1970. In the meantime metric and imperial scales will coexist but as more metric sheets become available we intend to replace all the extracts in this book to the new scales, styles and format. Further information about O.S. policy is contained in Leaflet No. 20 ' Metrication of Ordnance Survey Maps ' published October, 1969, by the Ordnance Survey at Southampton.

P.S.   A.H.C.C.   1970

CONTENTS

PART ONE: BASIC PRINCIPLES OF MAP READING

1. Scales and Marginal Information
page 1
Map Title; Map Scale; Metric Scales; Measurement of Distances; Conventional Signs; National Grid; Direction

2. Map Measurement
9
Measurement of Areas; Map Copying and Reduction

3. Representation of Relief
13
Contours; Trigonometrical Stations; Bench Marks and Spot Heights; Section Drawing; Intervisibility; Gradients

Questions on Part One
19

PART TWO: MAP INTERPRETATION

4. Recognition of Land Forms
20
Definitions of Common Landforms; The Landscape of River Erosion; Glaciated Highlands; Coastal Forms

5. The Identification of Rock-Types
25
The Permeable Rocks; The Impermeable Rocks; Igneous and Metamorphic Rocks; The Fenlands

6. Types of Settlement
31
Site; Situation; Function; Upland Settlements; Lowland Settlements; Coastal Settlements

7. Communications
38
Roads; Rivers, Canals; Railways; Air Communications; Description of a Route

8. Land Use
40
Farming; Woodland; Mineral Extraction; Industrial Use; Recreational Use; Waste Land

CONTENTS

PART THREE: ANALYSIS OF SELECTED MAPS AND MAP EXERCISES

9. Scarp and Vale: The Cotswolds (Map 1)   41

10. Fenland: The Middle Level (Map 2)   43

11. River Valleys and Coasts: Looe (Map 3)   44

12. Glaciated Highlands: The Lake District (Map 4)   46

13. A Limestone Upland: Ingleborough (Map 5)   48

14. Settlement and Communications:
    (A) Alloa (Map 6)   50
    (B) Aberystwyth (Map 7)   52

15. An Industrial Location: Skinningrove (Map 8)   53

Hints for the Examination   54

Ordnance Survey Symbols for 1 : 25,000 and 1 : 63,360   55

Questions on Part Three   56

16. Metric Map: Dorking (Map 9)   75

17. Metric Map: Exmouth (Map 10)   78

LIST OF FIGURES

1. Scales 1a. Imperial Scales *page* 2
   1b. Metric Scales 3
   1c. How to divide a line into equal parts 4
2. Method of measurement along a winding course 5
3a. The National Grid and Reference System 6
3b. How to give a Grid Reference 6
4. Compass Points 7
5. Direction on the map 7
5a. Direction on the map 7
5b. True North, Grid North, Magnetic North 7
5c. Relationship of Grid and Graticule 8
6. Measurement of Areas—by Squares Method 9
7. Measurement of Areas—by Strip Method 9
8a. Reduction to half-scale of Lake District map 10
8b. Reduction to half-scale of Looe map 10
9. Reduction of one-inch map to half-scale 11
10a and 10b. Methods of showing relief by Relief Drawing and Hachuring 13
10c and 10d. Methods of showing relief by Hill Shading and Contouring 13
11. Slope patterns 14
12a, 12b and 12c. Construction of a cross-section 15
13. A sketch-section 16
14. Cross-section to show geological structure of Ingleborough 17
15. Intervisibility and ' Dead Ground ' 18
16. The Horizontal Equivalent 18
17a and 17b. Slopes, Valleys and Spurs 21

18a and 18b. A Landscape of River Erosion *page* 21
19a. Scarp and Vale 22
19b. The Watershed 22
20. Characteristics of rivers and their valleys 23
21a and 21b. Glaciated Highlands 24
22a and 22b. Coastal Forms 24
23. The Water Table 25
24. Map of the Chalk Downland near Lewes 27
25a and 25b. Fen island and fen-line settlements 33
26. Confluence Town, Monmouth 35
27. Market Town, Melton Mowbray 35
28. Foot-hill settlement, Alva 36
29. Gap Town, Goring-on-Thames 36
30. Spring-line settlement, Wiltshire 37
31. Bridge Town, Bridgwater 37
32. Block diagram of Cotswolds map 42
33. Sketch-map showing position of West and East Looe 45
34. Sketch-map to show physical regions of the Lake District map 47
35. Block diagram of the Lake District map 47
36. Sketch-map to show physical regions of the Ingleborough map 48
37. Block diagram of Ingleborough map 49
38. Sketch-map of communications on map of Alloa 51
39. Sketch-map showing the site and situation of Aberystwyth 52
40. Geological section across North Downs 76

LIST OF PLATES AND MAPS

Plate 1. South Downs near Lewes

Plate 2. Fenland near Downham Market

Plate 3. The Looe Estuary

Plate 4. Lake District. Buttermere and Crummock Water

Plate 5. Ingleborough

Plate 6. Alva and the outskirts of Alloa

Plate 7. Aberystwyth

Plate 8. Skinningrove, north-east Yorkshire

Plate 9. Exmouth

Map 1. The Cotswolds: 1:63,360

Map 2. Fenland: 1:63,360

Map 3. Looe: 1:25,000

Map 4. Lake District: 1:63,360

Map 5. Ingleborough: 1:25,000

Map 6. Alloa, 1:63,360

Map 7. Aberystwyth: 1:25,000

Map 8. Skinningrove: 1:10,560

Map 9. Dorking: 1:50,000

Map 10. Exmouth: 1:25,000

PART ONE: BASIC PRINCIPLES OF MAP READING
Chapter One: Scales and Marginal Information

Map Title

Map reading begins by noting the name or title of the map. This may be the name of the most important settlement on the map, the name of the region covered by the map, e.g. The Lake District, or the name of an island if this comes conveniently within the compass of one sheet of the map series. On the map extracts given in examinations and on the flat issues of the six inch plan and the 1 : 25,000 map no title is usually given. On the folded maps published by official bodies such as the Ordnance Survey the title may be given on the front cover and on the spine.

The title gives the location of the map within the British Isles; the student should, at once, turn to the Atlas and refer the map to the wider setting of its regional geography.

The map usually carries numbers or letters that place it within the general framework of all the maps published in the same series at the same scale. By reference to the index diagram in the margin of the map sheet or to the cover of the folded maps any map can be located in this way and the adjacent sheets determined.

Map Scale

Now turn to the scale. Unless the student appreciates fully the meaning of scale it is impossible to read the map correctly. The successful representation of the very varied features of the earth's surface on a map is largely a question of scale. The map reader should be able to distinguish, by examining the scale, those features that are shown true to scale from those that are generalised or symbolised. He must cultivate the habit of checking the scale whenever a map is examined and will find that, with a little practice, the estimation of distances and areas on maps of different scales is not at all difficult. When travelling by cycle, car or on foot a map should always be carried and distances checked by comparing the mileages indicated on guide posts and milestones with those measured from the map. In this book there are examples of maps published by the Ordnance Survey on scales of one inch, six inches and about $2\frac{1}{2}$ inches to the mile.

Scale

This means ratio, proportion or relationship. Scale is the ratio of the distances and areas shown on the map to the corresponding distances and areas on the earth's surface. Let us examine the significance of scale on a map.

All the Ordnance Survey map extracts are overprinted with the National Grid. On the maps in this book the grid lines are spaced at intervals of one kilometre. Consider the size of a grid square on the six inch plan (the representation of the ground at six inches to the mile and on larger scales is usually called a plan), and compare to the sizes of the squares on the $2\frac{1}{2}$ inch and one inch maps. The square becomes progressively smaller on each map, although it represents the same area on the ground. On the one inch map the grid square is 1/36th the size of the square on the six inch plan. This must affect the amount of detail to be shown on the maps and the accuracy to which it can be drawn. Examine the detail in and around Skinningrove on the six inch plan and note the size and shape of buildings. The various types of buildings can be clearly distinguished; street names are given and the buildings alongside are obviously terraced houses. Schools and churches are drawn to plan and the detail of industrial plant, railway sidings and mines are fully shown. Large houses and farms are individually named; allotment gardens, tennis courts and many other features are picked out at this scale.

Next examine the $2\frac{1}{2}$ inch and one inch maps and compare similar features and the ways in which they are portrayed by the cartographer. For example, on these maps the churches are shown by symbols, the schools are named only on the $2\frac{1}{2}$ inch scale, and the details of railways and mines may be omitted altogether.

On six inch scales and larger the Ordnance Survey attempt to show all features true to the scale of the map; on the $2\frac{1}{2}$ inch and one inch maps generalisation of such natural features as rivers must be made and man-made features shown by symbols. On the one inch map a line 1/100 inch thick represents a distance of about 50 feet so that the map width of the symbol often greatly exceeds the width of the feature on the ground. Measure the widths of railways, roads, rivers (near the mouth and at intervals upstream), buildings, etc., on one inch and $2\frac{1}{2}$ inch maps and work out from the scale the actual distances in feet represented by these measurements.

On the one inch map Seventh Series, Ministry of Transport roads over 14 feet wide are shown by a symbol giving a ground representation of 163 feet. Very few roads come anywhere near to this width. On the $2\frac{1}{2}$ inch map the ground measurement of the Ministry of Transport road symbol is 60 feet and so some roads can be shown to scale.

Scale is commonly shown in three ways:

(I) *By a Statement*

one inch to a mile
six inches to a mile
ten miles to an inch
(NEVER one inch = one mile)

(II) *By a Representative Fraction, or R.F.*

This shows always one unit as the numerator. The denominator is the number of the same units on the ground represented by one unit on the map—e.g.

$\dfrac{1}{63,360}$ for a scale of one inch to a mile since there are 63,360 inches in a mile. This may also be shown as a ratio, 1 : 63,360.

The R.F. is perhaps the best way of showing scale since it avoids mention of any unit of measurement. European maps are constructed on the metric system and foreigners find confusing the British method of measurement. But with a known R.F. then a scale line can easily be drawn showing kilometres or any other national unit of measurement.

One use of the R.F. can be seen by reference to the $2\frac{1}{2}$ inch map. This map, popularly known as the $2\frac{1}{2}$ inch is actually drawn to the R.F. of 1 : 25,000, but this scale is not exactly $2\frac{1}{2}$ inches to the mile. A correct statement of scale would be calculated as follows:

25,000 inches on the ground are represented by one inch on the map.

$\therefore$ 63,360 inches (one mile) on the ground are represented by

$$\frac{63,360}{25,000} \text{ on the map.}$$

$$= 2.5344 \text{ inches.}$$

For a statement of scale of $2\frac{1}{2}$ inches to the mile the R.F. would be:

63,360 inches on the ground are represented by $2\frac{1}{2}$ inches on the map.

$\therefore$ One inch on the ground is represented by $63,360 \times \dfrac{2}{5}$

$$= 25,344 \text{ inches.}$$

The required R.F. is therefore 1 : 25,344.

Note that 1 : 25,000 is a larger scale than 1 : 25,344 and it would allow greater detail to be shown. The rule is: the higher the denominator of the R.F. the smaller the scale and, of course, the greater the area that can be shown on a map of given size.

(III) *By a Scale-line*

This is usually a plain scale of convenient length suitably marked into primary divisions with one division only marked into secondary divisions. This forms a backward-reading unit to the left of the zero mark, and complete subdivision of the forward-reading units is therefore avoided. The use of the scale is clear from Figs. 1a. and 1b.:

SCALES

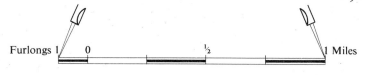

One Inch to One Mile or 1:63,360

Furlongs 1 / 0   1 Miles

About 2½ Inches to One Mile or 1:25,000

Furlongs 1 / 0   ½   1 Miles

Six Inches to One Mile or 1:10,560

1   0   ½   1
Furlongs   Miles

FIG 1a   The First Division of the Scale is a backward reading unit. The dividers are set to measure one mile, one furlong on each scale.

The scale-line is drawn in the lower margin of the one inch map and forms the border to the map on the 1 : 25,000 and six inch scales. It is represented in three forms: a scale of miles reading to furlongs, a scale in yards and feet, and a scale of kilometres reading to metres.

Metric Scales

With the gradual introduction of metric measurement scales will be shown by the scale-line and R.F. or ratio only, and the statement of scale will generally disappear along with the Imperial units of inches and miles. If conversion to miles and furlongs from kilometres is required, then direct measurment is possible from the scale-line itself which can be divided into both kilometre and mile units—see Maps 9 and 10. Many Ordnance Survey maps already have scales in decimal form, e.g. the large scale plans at 1 : 1,250 and 1 : 2,500, and the 1 : 25,000 medium scale map. Only the much used six inch plan (1 : 10,560) and the one inch map (1 : 63,360) are drawn to the traditional British scales. The six-inch plan will eventually be replaced completely by new plans published at 1 : 10,000 and it is anticipated that, in time, 1 : 50,000 maps will replace the one inch series. In both cases the new scales are larger than the old ones, and by using the scale ratios the amount of increase can be calculated as follows:

Scale of Imperial units – 1 : 10,560
Scale of Metric units – 1 : 10,000
Percentage increase in scale – $\dfrac{560 \times 100}{10,000} = 5.60\%$

Scale of Imperial units – 1 : 63,360

Scale of Metric units – 1 : 50,000
Percentage increase of scale – $\dfrac{13,360 \times 100}{50,000} = 26.72\%$

It is therefore clear that if the new maps cover the same area as the old ones the sheet sizes will be larger by 5.6 and 26.72 per cent respectively. In terms of practical measurement on a map this means:

On a scale of 1 : 63,360, 1 cm on the map represents 63,360 cm on the ground.

On a scale of 1 : 50,000, 1 cm on the map represents 50,000 cm on the ground.

Therefore, on the new metric map the enlargement of detail shown to scale is 63,360–50,000=approx. $\frac{1}{4}$ or 26.72% as above.

To appreciate the differences in area shown on the two scales compare the kilometre squares of the National Grid on the one inch extract, e.g. Map 1 and on the 1 : 50,000 extract, Map 9.

Scale Conversions

If a scale line is not given but the R.F. is known it is a simple matter to convert the map measurement into miles or kilometres as follows:

On a map scale 1 : 50,000 what is the ground distance represented by six inches on the map?

One inch on the map represents 50,000 inches on the ground.

∴ Six inches on the map represent $\dfrac{50,000 \times 6}{63,360}$ miles on the ground. $=4.73$ miles

METRIC SCALES

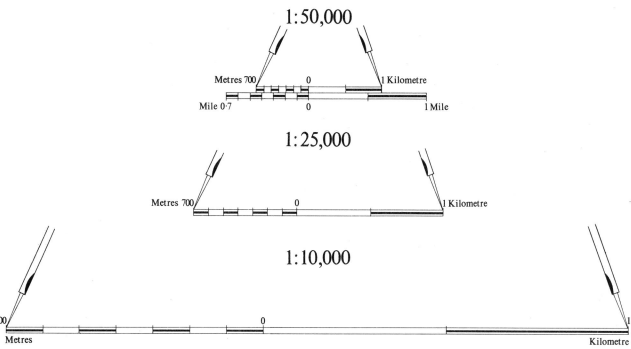

1:50,000

1:25,000

1:10,000

FIG. 1b   The dividers are set to measure 1.7 kilometres. (For comparison note the length of a line 1.7 miles on 1 : 50,000.)

On a map scale 1 : 25,000 what is the ground distance represented by ten centimetres on the map?

One centimetre on the map represents 25,000 cm on the ground.

$\therefore$ Ten centimetres on the map represent kilometres on the ground $\dfrac{25,000 \times 10}{100,000}$

$$= 2.5 \text{ kilometres}$$

Remember that two centimetres on the map represent one kilometre at the 1 : 50,000 scale and four centimetres represent one kilometre at the 1 : 25,000. For direct conversion of Imperial to metric measure the calculation is much more tedious:

$$1 \text{ kilometre} = 0.6214 \text{ mile}$$
$$1 \text{ mile} = 1.6093 \text{ kilometres}.$$

Construction of scale lines

In the period of change from traditional to fully metric scales some maps will be on one scale and others on the nearest metric equivalent so that one area might be covered only on the one inch scale whilst the adjacent sheet had been published at 1 : 50,000. For the convenience of measuring metric distances on the one inch map a scale divided into kilometre units should be constructed as illustrated in Figure 1b. Proceed as shown below. (There is, of course, no problem about constructing a scale line for a metric ratio provided a ruler marked in centimetres is to hand.)

In order to construct a scale line to represent 8 kilometres:

63,360 cm on the ground are represented by 1 cm on the map.

$8 \times 100,000$ cm (8 km) are represented by

$$\dfrac{800,000 \text{ cm on the map}}{63,360}$$

$$= 12.6 \text{ cm}$$

Draw a line this length and divide geometrically into eight equal parts, to represent the kilometre units, and, if desired, make further subdivision of the backward-reading unit to accommodate tenths of a kilometre. The method of dividing a line into any number of equal parts using a ruler and set square is shown below, Figure 1c.

Measurement of Distances

A pair of dividers should always be used to take straight-line measurements off the map. Pieces of cotton, string or wool may stretch and give a reading far from accurate. Compasses also are unsuitable since the pencil point may itself represent some fifty yards on the scale. Should the subdivision along the scale be inadequate for the accuracy of the measurement required, e.g. a distance to the nearest 100 yards on the $2\frac{1}{2}$ inch map-extract as used in examinations, then one must use the R.F. and convert the map measurement to ground measurement in the following manner:

What is the distance ' as the crow flies ' from Llangorwen church, grid reference 603838 to Llanbadarn church, grid reference 599810 on the map of Aberystwyth (Map VII), scale 1 : 25,000?

Distance taken from the map = 4.5 inches

Ground distance represented $= \dfrac{4.5 \times 25,000}{63,360} = \dfrac{112,500}{63,360}$

```
63,360) 112,500 (1 mile
         63,360
    36)  49,140 (1,365 yards
         36
        ___
         131
         108
        ___
         234
         216
        ___
         180
         180
        ___
         ...
```

$$= 1 \text{ mile } 1,365 \text{ yards}$$

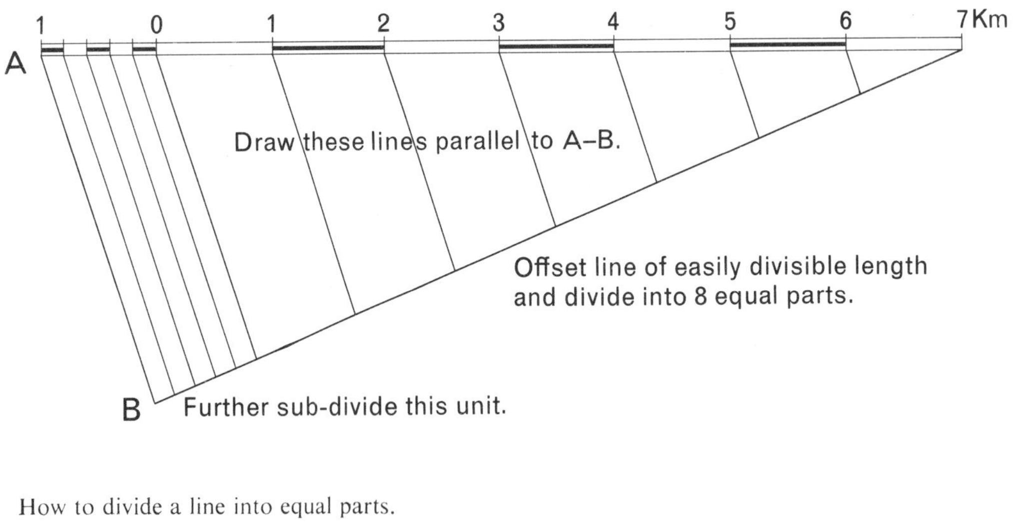

Scale line of 12·6 cm. representing 8 km.
Join end of scale line to end of offset line A–B.

Draw these lines parallel to A–B.

Offset line of easily divisible length and divide into 8 equal parts.

Further sub-divide this unit.

FIG. 1c   How to divide a line into equal parts.

Remember that on O.S. maps the normal grid lines are 1 km. apart. Straight-line distances east-west and north-south on these maps can be given very quickly in kilometres by counting the lines across the map or by consulting the grid numbers in the margins of the map.

Measurement along roads, railways and rivers

Distances along a winding road or river must be broken down into a series of short straight-line measurements, from bend to bend. A piece of strong cotton or thread could be used but the straight edge of a piece of stout paper is to be preferred.

Start with one corner of the paper, and at the end of each straight section, pivot the paper on a pencil point and rotate to the next straight section. This method avoids inaccuracies due to the free movement of the paper. See Figure 2.

When the measurements are complete apply the paper to the scale-line and read off the total distance.

For short measurements this method is quite satisfactory, but over longer distances errors are likely to occur as there will be bends in the roads and the rivers that the map-maker was unable to show because of the limitations of scale. This is particularly true on scales smaller than six inches to a mile.

Railway distances generally involve less difficulty since most railways follow more direct routes involving fewer bends and no sharp changes in direction.

A handy inexpensive map-measurer—the opisometer, can be obtained from most bookshops and stationers. This consists of a small wheel with counting dial calibrated in miles and kilometres. A pointer ticks up the distance as the measure is wheeled over the map. Always check the setting of the dial by first running over the scale line. If there is a discrepancy between the number on the dial and the values given on the scale-line, then after taking your measurement from the map run back the pointer to zero along the scale-line, noting from the scale-line the distance travelled. With cheaper models this may be necessary in any case since the counting dial may not be present.

Conventional Signs

The limitations of scale on a map should now be clear. Whenever it is impossible to show clearly, and to scale, any feature that is an important landmark, then the map-maker must choose a symbol or conventional sign to represent it. Many of these are familiar to all map-users: churches, railway-lines, roads, sand-pits and quarries, windmills, etc.

The regular map-user learns to recognise these signs by continual reference to map and landscape. The student is strongly recommended to check the map information in his home area and to prepare in his note-book lists of symbols and their meaning. The symbols can be divided into two major groups—

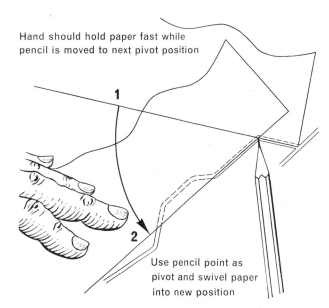

FIG. 2 Method of measurement along a winding course.

(i)   landscape features—e.g. symbols portraying communications, drainage, vegetation, buildings, mineral workings, etc.,

(ii) non-landscape features—e.g. boundary lines, latitude and longitude, methods of showing height, etc.

Characteristic sheets of the symbols used on O.S., $2\frac{1}{2}$ inch and one inch maps are given on page 55

National Grid

All post-war maps published by the Ordnance Survey are overprinted with a grid of kilometre squares that forms an excellent reference system to any place in the British Isles. The whole country is covered by primary squares of 100 kilometre side and these are subdivided into one kilometre secondary squares. For any place in the British Isles the same grid line intersection will appear on all the relevant maps published on different scales, so that no matter which map is used the grid reference will always be the same. The diagram Figure 3a explaining the origin of the National Grid should be studied carefully. A similar diagram, explaining the method of using the National Grid is given in the lower margin of all O.S. maps and this note is usually printed with the map extracts used for examination purposes.

The Grid numbers start from a point to the west of the Scilly Isles, and the position of any place can be given in terms of its distance east and north of this origin. The numbers running west to east along the top and bottom of the sheet are called Eastings; those running from south to north along the right and left margins are called Northings. When giving any reference always take first the Eastings numbers and then the Northings. Thus to refer to a kilometre square a

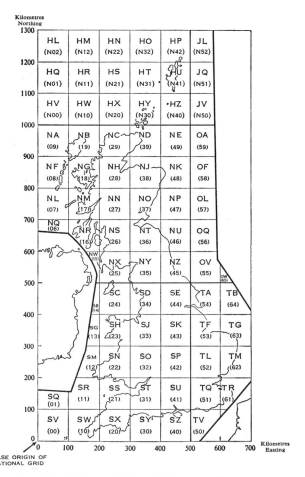

Fig. 3a.   The National Grid and Reference System.

four-figure reference can be given made up of the Easting and Northing bounding the square to the left and bottom—e.g. 5806 for the square containing Point A. in Figure 3b. This is the Normal Kilometre Reference.

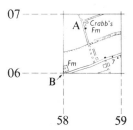

FIG. 3b.   How to give a grid reference.

For more precise location to within 100 metres a six-figure reference is needed. This is called the Normal National Grid Reference and is obtained by estimating the 'tenth' subdivisions of each square on the one inch map, but on the six inch and 1 : 25,000 maps a marginal strip is subdivided into these one hundred metre intervals. Both references would be repeated in each 100 kilometre square so that in order to make each reference unique the Grid Letters must also be

given. These are shown in Figure 3a and always prefix the normal reference to produce the Full Kilometre and Full National Grid References. They will apply to one square and one point only in the British Isles.

On map extracts and around the margin of the map sheets the letters may be missing and it is then necessary to use the small figures printed in the map corners. (These numbers appear in the appropriate squares below the letter in Figure 3a).

Points A and B in Figure 3b are taken from the one inch Fenland sheet (Map 2) and can be used to demonstrate the different ways of giving a map reference.

Point A.   Normal National Grid Reference 583068
Point A.   Full National Grid Reference TF/583068
                                      or 53/583068
Point B.   Normal National Grid Reference 580060
Point B.   Full National Grid Reference TF/580060
                                      or 53/580060

The Full Kilometre Reference to the grid square on the map is TF/5806.

Direction

Direction is studied best with the map and compass in the field. The student should take a one inch map of his home district and climb the nearest summit. This may be a church tower or the top of a high building in flat country. The map must be set by identifying at least three prominent features in the landscape with the corresponding features on the map. Taking the top of the map as north one can obtain the general direction of the compass. If a hand compass is available it is possible to set the map more accurately. If the legend in the lower margin of the map-sheet is consulted the angular differences between Grid North, True North and Magnetic North, in the four corners of the map can be found. The compass points to Magnetic North so thet the map must be moved round until the compass needle coincides with Magnetic North on the map. Allowance must be made for the annual variation of Magnetic North from True North at the point of observation.

Figure 5b shows a typical direction indicator found in the lower margin of Ordnance Survey maps. The differences between Magnetic North, Grid North, and True North may be stated as follows:

Magnetic North—the direction in which a compass needle points.
Grid North   —the direction of the grid lines on the map.
True North   —the direction of the north pole.
At the present time the Magnetic North Pole lies to

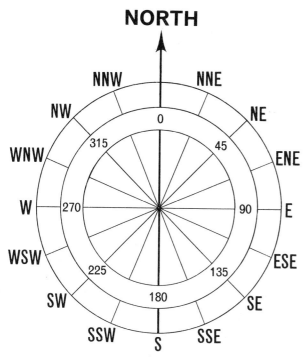

FIG. 4 Compass points.

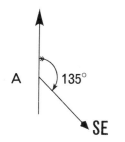

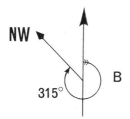

FIG. 5a Direction on the map. Direction from B to A is north-west, and direction of B from A is south-east. But direction between A and B must be north-west-south-east.

the west of the True North Pole as seen from the British Isles and the difference between the poles is best expressed in degrees. This difference is the magnetic variation and it will, of course, vary from place to place on the earth's surface, even within the area shown on a one inch map, so that the value given for it usually indicates the variation at the centre of the map. A further complication arises because the magnetic variation changes also with time and so the annual variation of the compass at any point must also be known. This is why the procedure outlined above must be followed if a correct compass bearing or accurate setting of the map is to be achieved.

Direction can also be found on all Ordnance Survey maps by examining the meridians of longitude and the parallels of latitude. On the whole sheets the map border shows the values of latitude and longitude and with a ruler it is possible to join up the corresponding points across the map to produce a network of meridian and parallels called a map graticule. Map extracts, however, do not contain these points and such a construction is not really necessary in any case as the map contains, here and there, a small lightly drawn cross which marks the intersection of the lines of latitude and longitude at that point. An example of such an intersection can be seen at Grid Reference 114335 on Map 1. The upright line points true north and is part of a meridian which intersects the true North Pole, and the horizontal line runs truly east to west. Note that the Grid Lines do not, at any point, correspond with these graticule lines so that they only give a very general indication of direction—see Figure 5c.

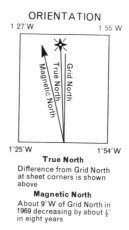

FIG. 5b True North, Grid North, Magnetic North.

For indicating direction in examination answers it is generally satisfactory to use the points of the compass. Measurement in degrees is not usually required. Figure 4 shows sixteen points of the compass with the corresponding angular bearings. Note that bearings are given as part of the 360 ° of the full circle, reckoned clockwise from magnetic north. There should be no confusion over giving a bearing if one remembers that direction is given *from* one place *to* another—e.g. in Figure 5a.

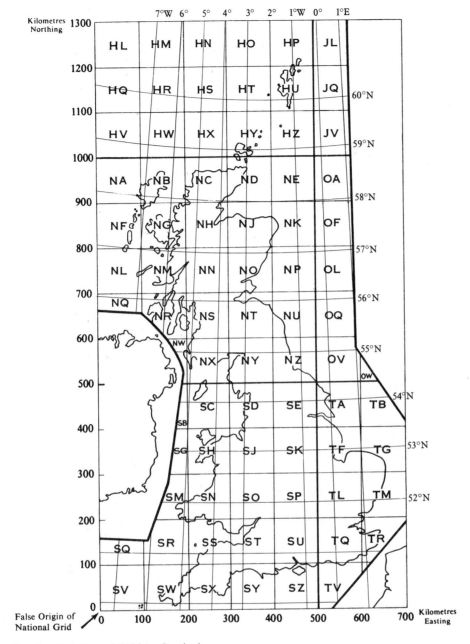

Fig 5c   Relation of Grid to Graticule.

Chapter Two: Map Measurement

Measurement of Areas

If we wish to calculate the area of land or of sea, or perhaps of a lake, or the extent of woodland shown on the map, simple graphic methods can be employed.

The Squares Method

Transfer to tracing paper an outline of the area to be measured and cover with small squares, all the same size. In the example, Figure 6 below, taken from Map 4 of the Lake District, quarter inch squares have been drawn. On this tracing of the one inch map each square will represent $\frac{1}{16}$th square mile. Place a tick in each complete square as you proceed. Those squares that are broken by the map outline can be dealt with by a 'give-and-take' method—e.g. in Figure 6 count square A as a complete square and cancel square B. The land has been 'taken' from B and 'given' to A to make the whole square. Account for all the other 'broken' squares in the same way, count the number of ticks and convert to square measure. For an approximate answer in square kilometres this method could be applied directly to the map by counting the grid squares.

The Strip Method

Use strips of equal width instead of squares as in the previous example. The 'give-and-take' principle is applied in the same way to both ends of each strip but it is easier to apply, because the 'broken' areas are so much smaller. To obtain the total area, add together the lengths of all the strips and multiply by the width of one strip. See Figure 7.

The success of both these methods depends on the care taken in tracing the map outline and the skill in applying the 'give-and-take' method.

On large scale plans such as those drawn to scales of 1 : 2,500 and 1 : 1,250 the area of parcels of land is given in acres. On the new and revised sheets at this scale now published in metric form the area of these land parcels is stated in hectares to three decimal places as well as in acres. When, eventually, the medium and small scale maps (e.g. the 1 : 25,000 and the one inch) are published in fully metric form then the calculation of areas in square miles will be an obsolete task. We need then only make use of squares or strips based on the kilometre grid.

AREAS

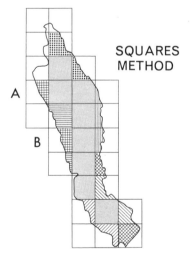

SQUARES
METHOD

A

B

Approximate area of Crummock Water = one square mile
(16 squares ¼ ml x ¼ = ¹⁶/₁₆ sq. mls.)

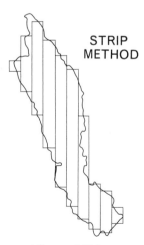

STRIP
METHOD

Approximate area of Crummock Water = one square mile
(¹²⁵/₁₆ x ¹/₈ = ¹²⁵/₁₂₈ sq. mls.)

FIG. 6   The shading indicates the complementary squares.

FIG. 7   The total length of all strips is 125/16 inches and the width of each strip is $\frac{1}{8}$ inch.

Map Copying and Reduction

Every student should be able to copy a map and to reduce it to a given fraction of its original scale. He can then transfer selected detail from the published map to his own sketch map, keeping an overall accuracy of scale. Examination questions frequently ask the candidate to reduce a map to half-scale and to insert the principal relief and drainage features or some detail of the human geography.

As such great care has been taken over scale in plotting the original map any sketch map used in map analysis is obviously better drawn to scale than roughed out freehand. With a little practice copying and reduction can be done quickly and accurately. All the map figures in this book have been drawn to scale and this is indicated either by the representative fraction or by a statement below each one. Figures 8a and 8b are examples of half scale reductions.

Copying

The copying of a map is best done on tracing paper but this method may be forbidden in the examination room. An alternative method makes use of the kilometre grid covering the map by marking off the grid line intervals along the edge of a piece of paper. Measure the external dimensions of the sheet and rule and number the grid lines. Select the features to be shown, note where they cross the grid lines on the map and draw in the corresponding position on the sketch.

Reduction of the one-inch map to half-scale

This can be carried out in a similar way. Figure 8a is a reduction to half scale of the one inch map of the Lake District (Map 4), to show the main drainage features. Note that only the alternate grid lines appear on the reduced map so that four squares on the original are represented by one square on the sketch. It will be seen that the distance between the lines on the reduction is the same as between the grid lines on the map but they are numbered differently. Notice, however, that often the margins of the map extract are not grid lines but lines falling somewhere between. These odd strips should be dealt with first, measuring their width with a ruler, halving them, and transferring them to the sketch. If the number of squares along the margins of the map extract is also odd, the odd ones, too, should also be halved and transferred. On the one inch reduction when adding detail concentrate on four of the map squares at a time, covering the rest with sheets of loose paper.

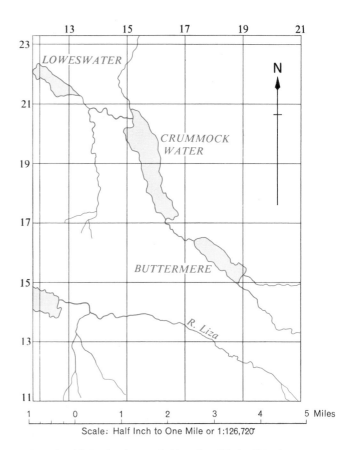

Scale: Half Inch to One Mile or 1:126,720

FIG. 8   (a) Reduction to half-scale of Lake District map.

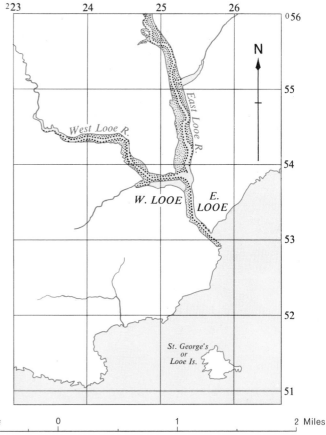

Scale: 1:50,000 or about 1¼ Inches to One Mile

FIG. 8   (b) Reduction to half-scale of Looe map.

In a class, or at home, a sheet of paper with a ' window ' square cut from the middle is very useful in transferring features from map extract to sketch. An example of the method is given in Figure 9, for a scale reduction of the one inch map.

To cut the ' window ' simply fold your paper across the middle and lay it on the map, ticking the width of two grid squares near the centre of the paper. Cut down each tick to the length of one square and cut across. Unfold the paper to reveal a window the exact size of four of the map squares.

Reduction of the 2½ inch map to half-scale

After the difficulties of the one inch reduction the 2½ inch presents little trouble. The grid squares on the map are large enough to be individually reduced. As in the case of the one inch the main map extract should be reduced first, any odd marginal strips dealt with next and the full squares last. No actual measurement is necessary, however, for any process. The margins of the 2½ inch map carrying divisions in grid ' tenths '. If these are counted and subdivided very accurate lengths can then be set off with a pair of dividers without the use of a ruler except for the drawing of straight lines. *Note* that grid numbering on the 2½ inch sketch will be the same as on the extract and detail will be transferred to the reduction square by square. Figure 8b of the Looe 2½ inch map has been reduced to half scale and this reduction should be consulted.

Enlargement of the map may be carried out in the same way but satisfactory results are not possible because of the scale difficulties. We have seen already

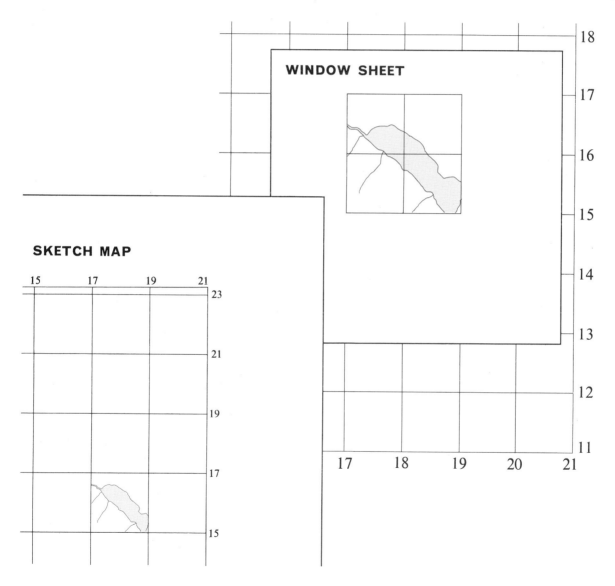

FIG. 9   Reduction of one-inch map to half-scale.

that on small scales much detail is generalised or shown by symbols. It is clearly impossible to make an accurate enlargement of such features.

No sketch map, enlargement or reduction is complete without a title, north arrow, and simple short scale-line to indicate the new scale, or this may be given as the new representative fraction.

Chapter Three: Representation of Relief

A

B

C

D

Fig. 10 Methods of showing relief.

Map extracts showing the town of Swaffham, Norfolk.

A. Relief drawing in the style of the Elizabethan maps.

B. Hachures in the style of the Ordnance Survey one-inch First Edition.

C. Hill shading and contours in the style of the Ordnance Survey one-inch Third Edition *(without colour)*.

D. Contours only, in the style of the Ordnance Survey one-inch Seventh Edition *(without colour)*.

Relief is the shape of the ground surface and a good method of relief portrayal must show not only the height of the land but also its shape and gradient, so that individual land forms can easily be recognised. The best method for topographical maps is undoubtedly the contour which combines height and slope. Earlier methods were chiefly pictorial and inaccurate. Until accurate surveying instruments were invented no other methods were possible.

One of the earliest techniques was Relief Drawing where hills were drawn in profile and lightly shaded to suggest height and bulk. Other shading methods assume a light shining obliquely on the landscape so that some slopes are in shadow and others unshaded are in the light. Yet another technique is by hachures—lines drawn on the map in the direction of the steepest slope and the steeper the slope the closer are the hachures drawn.

These methods of representing relief all suffer from the loss of accuracy in the detail required by modern maps unless supported by another technique such as the contour line. Moreover, the density of the shading on drawings is often such that it obscures other detail and makes overprinting of names extremely difficult. Comparisons of these techniques with the contour can be seen in Figures 10a, b, c and d.

In this book the maps show relief by contours, trigonometrical points, bench marks and spot heights. In the special one inch Tourist Edition of the Lake District (Map 4) selected contours are chosen to mark the divisions between coloured layers, the colours ranging light to dark from low to high ground. This system of layer-colouring is used to great effect in the small-scale maps of most atlases. On the Lake District extract the layer-colouring is supplemented by oblique hill-shading, assuming the source of light near the ground in the north-west.

A map has two dimensions only; the third dimension, height must be shown pictorially so that the form of the land can be read at a glance by the experienced map user. The only true representation of relief would be on a plaster or plastic model.

Contours

A contour may be defined as a line on a map joining all points the same height above Ordnance Survey Datum Level. For the present map issues published by the Ordnance Survey ordnance datum is the mean sea-level recorded at Newlyn in Cornwall. The interval between successive contours should remain constant on any one map sheet, and on all maps published in one edition. On O.S. maps the contour interval is 50 feet on the one inch map and 25 feet on the 1 : 25,000 and the six inch map. This is known as the Vertical Interval or V.1. To assist the map reader, contour lines are thickened at regular intervals: every 250 feet on the one inch map and every 100 feet on the 1 : 25,000. Any confusion arising out of contour reading should readily be removed if it is remembered that to walk along a contour would be to follow a level path, and by leaving the

contour one must rise or fall.

The geographer is closely concerned with slopes and land forms. Where contour lines are close together the slopes are steep, and conversely where the lines are distantly spaced the slopes are gentle. If the contour lines are spaced at regular intervals the slope is even. The closer the contour lines the more the slope angle approaches 90 degrees. If the slope is vertical the contour lines will merge, e.g. in sea-cliffs and quarry faces. Slope patterns produced by actual ground surfaces are shown in Figure 11.

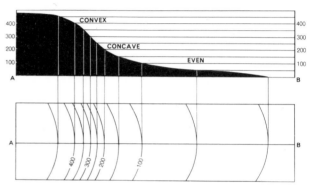

FIG. 11 Slope patterns.

The limitation of the contour is seen on the Fenland map (Map 2) with its V.I. of 50 feet. On this sheet most of the land is below 50 feet with only two contours appearing on the edge of map and the relative differences of height (so important in a low lying area) are then shown by selected spot heights.

Trigonometrical Stations, Bench Marks and Spot-Heights

These are points accurately surveyed and shown as heights above mean sea-level by points on the map, with the actual height in feet appearing on the map by the side of all spot heights and selected trigonometrical stations.

Trigonometrical points or stations

Distances are surveyed by angular measurements and the ground distance calculated by trigonometry. The surveyors erect concrete pillars on the summits of the hills which act as the corners of the main triangles of the Survey. Church towers and other high buildings are also used. These are the trigonometrical stations seen on the maps and they can be used for revision of detail at any time.

Bench Marks

These may be found cut in 'benches' usually walls, gate-posts or the sides of buildings. The height of each bench-mark above sea-level has been accurately determined by a levelling process to within 1/100th of a foot though the decimal places are not given on the small-scale and medium-scale maps included in this book.

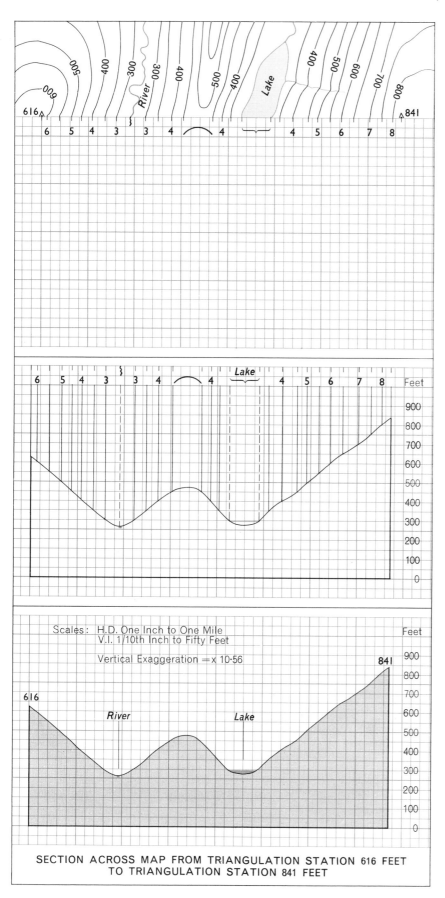

SECTION ACROSS MAP FROM TRIANGULATION STATION 616 FEET
TO TRIANGULATION STATION 841 FEET

FIG. 12a Rule in pencil a line linking the two ends of the section. Place the edge of the graph paper along the line of section so as to position neatly your profile in relation to the sheet as a whole. Tick off the crossing points of contours and label with the correct height. Also carefully mark the position and extent of other features, e.g. rivers, lakes, etc.

FIG. 12b Draw base line equal in length of section by dropping guiding verticals from the end ticks. Choose a suitable vertical scale and raise the ends of the section at least 50 feet above the highest contour, cut by the line of section. Drop vertical guide lines from each tick along the margin to correct height on section profile. Join up the lower ends of the lines to produce a smooth final profile.

FIG. 12c Tidy up the section profiles by rubbing out all guide lines. Label clearly important features. Attach title, details of scales; colour land and water features.

Spot-Heights

There is no physical evidence of spot-heights in the field but they appear frequently on maps, along roads and between contours and near sea-level to aid interpretation between the contour interval and are shown thus — .431.

Section Drawing
A cross-section

The shape of the land surface is brought out very well by the construction of a vertical section along a line drawn on the map. Significant breaks of slope may be revealed on the section that otherwise would be hidden from the map observer. The section may be annotated to indicate important features of drainage or land-use. An example of a cross section taken from the map of Ingleborough (Map 5) is given in Figure 14.

Method

Take the edge of a piece of graph paper and mark carefully where the contours cross the line of section. Number the contours as shown in Figure 12a. Erect a vertical scale to your section-block choosing an interval that does not give too great a vertical exaggeration. For the one inch map a scale of 1/10 inch to represent 50 feet is quite suitable. In upland regions there is really no need for the vertical scale to start at sea-level. Keep the horizontal scale the same as that of the map. Drop vertical lines as shown in Figure 12b (with experience lines on the graph paper can be used) to the heights along the section and join up by a smooth line. Shade the section to give the impression of solidity, and finally give a title to the section and indicate the scales used. See Figure 12c.

The vertical exaggeration on a section can be calculated as follows:

On one inch map R.F. is 1 : 63,360

$\therefore$ 1/10 inch on map represents 6,336 inches = 528 feet

Let 1/10 inch represent 50 feet on the vertical scale

Then vertical exaggeration $= \dfrac{528}{50} = 10.56$

A sketch-section

Measure the length of the section and construct a section block. The line of section may be drawn in by eye estimating the rise and fall of land, from careful inspection of the contours. Such a profile can be drawn in an examination when there is no time to carry out the detailed procedure of the cross-section. Although no fixed vertical scale is used, some indication of height along the profile is desirable. An example of this kind of section taken off the map of Aberystwyth (Map 7) is given in Figure 13. Always fix the section by quoting grid references at both ends.

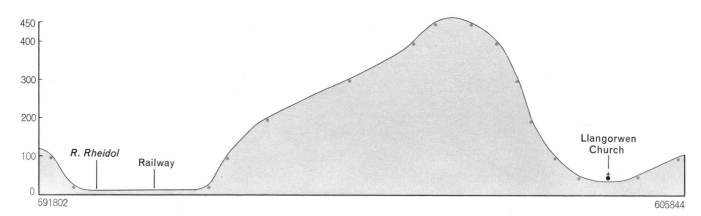

FIG. 13   Sketch-section across Aberystwyth sheet from Tynrabbi Chapel. 605844 to Penparcau 591802.
Contours plotted at marked breaks of slope.
Vertical scale 1/10th inch to 25 feet.

Intervisibility

Section drawing can be used effectively to discover whether two points are intervisible and to reveal 'dead ground'. A series of sections can be made to show the total area visible to an observer from one hill top. In Figure 15 drawn from the map of the Looe district (Map 3) the observer at Trigonometrical Station G.R. 231533 would see clearly to the next Trigonometrical Station G.R. 261542, but most of the estuary and the two rivers, the West and East Looe, would be hidden from view and constitute 'dead ground'.

Gradients

The degree of slope or gradient of stretches of roads, rivers, hill and valley-sides can be measured directly from the map. Gradient is expressed as a proportion, the vertical distance in terms of the forward distance: e.g. 1 in 10; 1 in 20; 1 in 30, etc. A vertical face would have a gradient of 1 in 0 and a horizontal surface of 0 in 1. The vertical and horizontal units must always be the same so that on O.S. maps the horizontal units must be converted to feet. To obtain the gradient along a road or hill-side, measure the forward distance between the top and bottom of the slope and convert to feet. Then calculate the difference in height between the two points from the contour values and by simple division the gradient is determined. An example is worked out overleaf. Note that on the one inch and 1 : 25,000 maps a single arrow is placed across roads with gradients 1 in 7 to under 1 in 5, and a double arrow where the gradient is 1 in 5 or steeper.

It must be pointed out, however, that the method described above contains an inherent error since the forward distance measured is not the slope distance but the horizontal equivalent. The error is negligible except in truly mountainous country—e.g. for a slope of 1 : 15 the error on the map is only 0.2%.

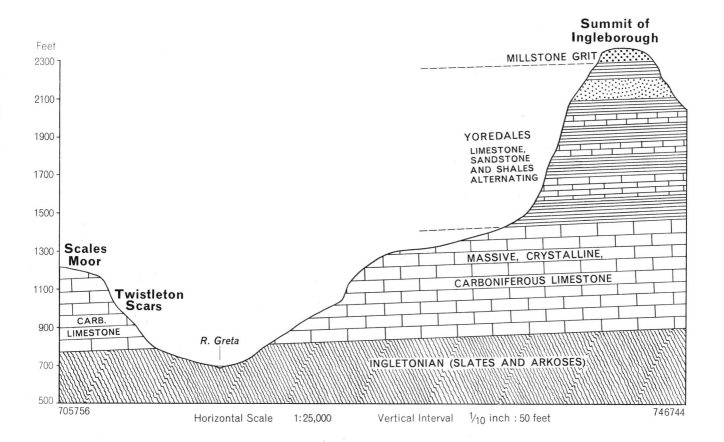

FIG. 14   Cross-section to show geological structure of Ingleborough.

The Horizontal Equivalent

All slope measurements taken by surveyors in the field are reduced to the horizontal equivalent and ultimately to mean sea-level. It is as though all the distances were taken along a plane at sea-level. The meaning of Horizontal Equivalent can be seen from the diagram, Figure 16.

The distance shown on the map will be AB and not AC, the surveyed and actual distance. In regions of subdued relief the differences will be slight and can be ignored; but in mountainous country keep the horizontal equivalent always in mind when climbing. If you set out to walk to the top of Pillar Mountain (171121) from the Youth Hostel (195123) on the map of the Lake District (Map 4) and allow for the reduced speed of ascent, you will underestimate your time of arrival unless you remember that the measured distance is short of the actual distance to be covered.

Calculation of Gradient from Map IV

Calculate the gradient of the footpath from Crag Houses G.R. 174172 to the summit of Whiteless Pike G.R. 180189.

Distance by footpath, i.e. horizontal distance

$$= 6,600 \text{ feet}$$

Difference in height, i.e. vertical distance $= 1,709$ feet

$$\text{Average Gradient} = \frac{1,709}{6,600}$$

$$= 1 : 3.8$$

i.e. *approximately* 1 : 4

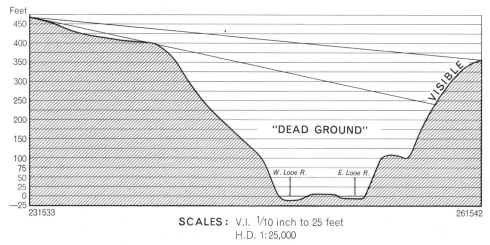

SCALES: V.I. $^1/_{10}$ inch to 25 feet
H.D. 1:25,000

FIG. 15 Intervisibility and 'dead ground'.

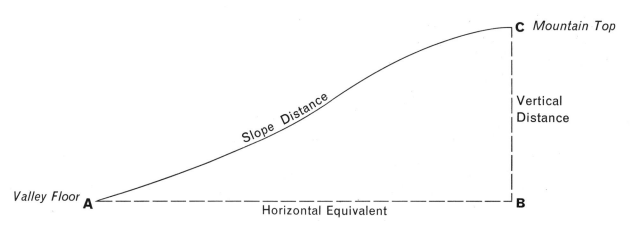

FIG. 16 The horizontal equivalent.

Questions on Part One

1. State to two decimal places how many inches to the mile are equivalent to an R.F. of 1 : 25,000.
2. Construct a scale line at 1 : 10,560 to read to the nearest 100 yards.
3. What distances on the ground are represented by the following measurements taken from a map R.F. 1 : 25,000:
   1. 13.7 inches
   2. 8.6 inches
   3. 1.5 inches
4. Measure the distances by road on the one inch Fenland Sheet (Map 2) between the parish churches of Downham Market 613033 and Outwell 513037.
5. Measure the distance by rail on the Fenland Sheet (Map 2) between Downham Market Station and Stow Bardolph Station.
6. Measure the distance by river on the Looe Sheet (Map 3) (following the middle of the channel) from the harbour mouth to the highest point to which Ordinary Tides flow on the West Looe River.
7. State the direction in degrees and by the points of the compass of the following features from the summit of the Red Pike on the Lake District Sheet (Map 4): Pillar Mountain (171121); Iron Crag (126120); Gatesgarth (194150); Crabtree (131215); Robinson (202168).
8. List all the O.S. symbols and their meanings appearing in grid squares 2355 on the Looe Sheet (Map 3) and 9192 on the Alloa Sheet (Map 6).
9. Calculate the area of land shown on the maps of Looe and Alloa (Maps 3 and 6).
10. Reduce to half-scale the map areas limited by grid lines as follows: (a) On Fenland map (Map 2)—eastings 56 to 61 and northings 06 to 10. (b) On Cotswolds map (Map 1)—eastings 00 to 04 and northings 33 to 37. Insert all details shown by symbols and give reduced scale-line and new R.F.
11. Reduce to one third the scale, the map areas limited by grid lines as follows:
    (a) On Abertstwyth map (Map 7)—eastings 58 to 60 and northings 82 to 84.
    (b) On Looe map (Map 3)—eastings 240 to 266 and northings 509 to 530. Draw in coastline, contours at 100 feet intervals, and insert rivers. Add new R.F.
12. Consult the Lake District map (Map 4) and list the various ways in which height and relief are shown in grid square 1615.
13. What are the advantages and disadvantages of the methods of showing relief by hill-shading used on the Lake District map (Map 4)?
14. Keeping the horizontal scale the same as the map and using a vertical scale of 1/10 inch to 50 feet construct on graph paper cross-sections along:
    (i) Grid line easting 60 on the Aberystwyth map (Map 7),
    (ii) Grid line easting 87 on the Alloa map (Map 6).
    Indicate important features crossed by the line of section.
15. Draw a sketch-section along grid line northing 35 on the Cotswolds map (Map 1), marking the river, railway and main road.
16. Determine whether you could see Dumbleton church 017357 from the church at Snowshill 096337 on the Cotswold map (Map 1).
17. Draw a sketch-map using Map 1 to show how much of the small hill at Dumbleton is visible from Broadway church—095373. (At least two inter-visibility sections will be necessary.)
18. Calculate the average gradient from Crina Bottom 723735 by the footpath to the summit of Ingleborough Hill, on Map 5.
19. The road from Newlands Hause to Buttermere village on the Lake District map (Map 4) shows three separate gradient symbols. By calculation check the O.S. symbols and state the actual gradients.
20. To what destination would the Post Office send letters addressed simply by the following grid references? All necessary maps are in this book; the first two figures are references to the 100 kilometre squares and appear in the margins of the map extracts.
    1. The Rector   42/068343
    2. The Warden   35/195124
    3. The Manager   34/717753
    4. The Registrar   22/581817
    5. The Secretary   53/618013
    6. The Laird   26/935979
    7. The Head Teacher   20/263555
21. Draw scale lines of kilometres for maps shown on the one inch and six inch scales to measure 10 kilometres and 3 kilometres respectively, sub-dividing the back-reading unit to show metres.
22. Construct a section across Map 9—to show the main relief features between spot height 72 metres 086533 and the trigonometrical station at 179535.

PART TWO: MAP INTERPRETATION
Chapter Four: Recognition of Land Forms

The extent to which the student can pass from map-reading to the correct map interpretation of land forms is dependent on his knowledge of physical geography. In all examinations in Geography for General Certificate of Education, questions are set on this branch of the subject and the candidate should be acquainted with the more important processes of land sculpture that mould the face of the earth. In this chapter only the briefest mention of these processes can be given. The requirements of the syllabus at Ordinary Level are covered in *Physical Geography*—H. R. Cain. A Certificate Series, Longmans, 1961, and students are referred to this work.

The surface features of the earth are the product of two sets of forces, those acting within the earth's crust and those acting at the surface. Forces acting within the crust are responsible for the general shape or outline of the major land forms, but in Britain and in many other landscapes, the external forces of rivers, ice, wind and the waves of the sea are more significant in moulding the present-day features. At the present time in Britain the principal agents of erosion are fast-flowing rivers and the waves continually breaking on our shores, but a map of any Highland region will give some indication of the work of ice in the form of valley glaciers that were present during the last Ice Age, and even in lowland areas there is often a thick mantle of glacial deposits obscuring the form of the underlying rocks.

In describing the physical features of the map, use must always be made of the special technical vocabulary learned in the lessons on physical geography. Avoid a general description in loose colloquial style. The more common features to be seen on Ordnance Survey maps are listed below with definitions adapted from *Glossary of Geographical Terms*, Compiled by a Committee of the British Association, edited by L. Dudley Stamp, Longmans, 1961.

Definitions of Common Landforms

Col: A marked depression in a line of mountains or hills.

Escarpment: A landform with sides sloping in opposite directions consisting of a steep scarp slope and a more gentle dip or back slope. Highest part is called the crest. The term cuesta is now widely used to describe the same feature. (Cotswolds Map I and Figure 19a).

Floodplain: A plain bordering a river formed of deposits of sediments carried down by a river.

Hill: An elevation generally under 2,000 feet.

Knoll: A small hill, more or less rounded in form.

Mountain: A natural elevation of the earth's surface rising more or less abruptly—generally over 2,000 feet in Britain. It may terminate in a marked summit.

Pass: Col or saddle providing a route-way through a line of hills. It may be at a high or low level.

Plateau: An elevated tract of comparatively flat or level land. When cut up by streams it is a 'dissected plateau'.

Ridge: A long and narrow stretch of elevated ground.

River-Basin: The area drained by a river and its tributaries.

Saddle: A similar depression to the col but generally higher, broader and sloping more gently from the summit.

Spur: A projection of land from high to low ground.

Valley: A long depression between stretches of high ground usually occupied by a stream. If streamless it is a 'dry valley'.

Watershed or water-parting: The line separating the headwaters of rivers flowing in different directions. It may or may not coincide with the crest-line of the relief. See Figure 19b.

On the map we must learn to recognise the characteristic land forms by interpreting the contour patterns and the other methods used of showing relief. In the remainder of this chapter block diagrams accompanied by contour sketches illustrate the most common British land forms and all references to them are given in bold type.

The Landscape of River Erosion
Slopes, Valleys and Spurs

The most common and the most easily identified landforms are **valleys** and **spurs**. Figures 17a and 17b show the shape taken by the contours of typical examples of these features. A valley is immediately recognised if it is occupied by a river, but a dry valley may be mistaken by the inexperienced map-reader for a spur, as the contour patterns are the same. Any difficulty is removed by consulting the contour values and it will be seen that in the valley the contours bend back up-valley in the shape of a 'V'; in the spur the 'V' is towards lower ground. The recognition of slopes as **convex, concave** and **even** has been discussed in Chapter 3, Figure 11. These are shown along a spur in Figure 17b, concave along the lower slope, an even section in the middle, and convex on the upper slope; this form is

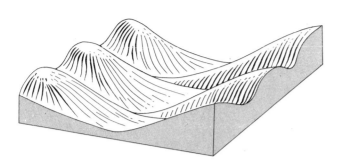

FIG. 17   (a) Slopes, valleys and spurs.

FIG. 18   (a) A landscape of river erosion.

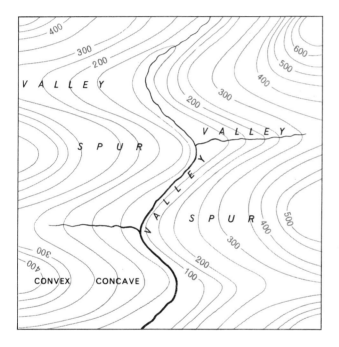

FIG. 17 (b)

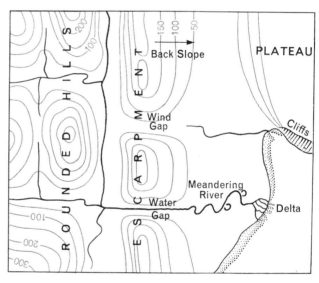

FIG. 18 (b)

frequently found in nature. Make a list of the many excellent examples to be found on the Looe map (Map III).

Plateaus, Cuestas, Scarp and Vale

The block diagram, Figure 18a, accompanying contoured map, Figure 18b, show these related landforms. They occur in regions of unfolded rocks that have been raised above sea-level and are undergoing erosion. The rocks are usually sedimentary (e.g. limestone, sandstone, shale), though lava plateaus are also known, as in the plateau of Antrim, Northern Ireland. Where the rock strata lies more or less horizontal the land may appear

as a flat-topped plateau. Where the rocks are gently inclined the weaker rocks will be removed by weathering and river erosion more rapidly than the resistant ones which frequently stand out boldly in a **scarp face,** rising to the **crest** of the **escarpment** and falling more gently down the **dip** or **back slope**. The true dip slope is the angle which the actual rock strata makes with the horizontal and few true dip slopes are found in the landscape. The term back slope is to be preferred. The differences between the true dip slope and the more common back slope are illustrated in Figure 19a. The combined land form of the scarp and back slope is known as a **cuesta** or **escarpment**. The lowland, often wide and extensive, at the foot of the scarp, is called a

vale and many examples can be seen in Britain, e.g. The Vale of Evesham beyond the **scarp edge** on the map of the Cotswolds. (Map 1.)

Water and Wind Gaps

These are often of considerable importance as they provide routeways through ranges of hills. **Water gaps** are seen at once by the roads and railways using them, running alongside the river. **Wind gaps** are similar features, once occupied by rivers but now abandoned except perhaps for a minor stream or patch of marshland. See Figures 18a and 18b and 19a.

Cols, Passes and Saddles

All three are found in mountain regions and may owe their origin to ice action subsequently smoothed in outline by weathering and stream erosion, but frequently result from the cutting back of streams on either side of the watershed. They may be the only means of access from one valley to another and are used by trackways, roads and occasionally by railways. Good examples can be found on the Lake District map. (Map 4.)

River Valleys

Ordnance Survey maps are most valuable in showing the varied features of river erosion and deposition. According to features which are present we can recognise the stage of development reached by the river and its valley.

Youthful Valleys

Fast-moving streams erode rapidly the rocks they cross, creating deep, steep-sided **V-shaped valleys,** and are said to be in the **Stage of Youth.** The long profile of such streams will show irregularities where harder bands of rock outcrop, and waterfalls or rapids may result. See Maps 3 and 4 and Fig. 20.

Mature Valleys

Mature rivers erode laterally and their valley cross-section is more open, the summits rounded and the valley floor wider than in youth. The river will swing from side to side, undercutting **river cliffs** on the outside and building up mudbanks and water meadows on the inside of its bends. See Fig. 20.

Old-Age Valleys

The **senile river** has great volume, carrying seawards a heavy load of rock particles. Only a little erosion is now carried on and there is much deposition along the banks of the river and across the broad **flood plain.** **Ox-bow lakes** indicate old river courses and the valley floor, contained in low, smoothed hills is wider than the belt of present meandering. In Fig. 20, the main characteristics are shown, but it should be noted that

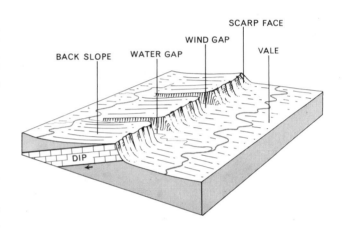

FIG. 19 (a) Scarp and vale. The diagram illustrates the relationship between true rock dip and the back slope of the escarpment.

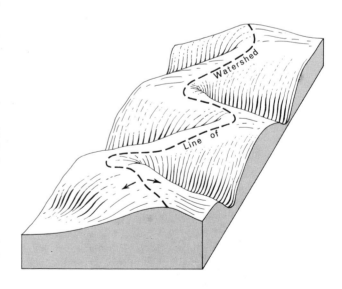

FIG. 19 (b) The Watershed. Streams cutting back into the upland have produced a zig-zag line.

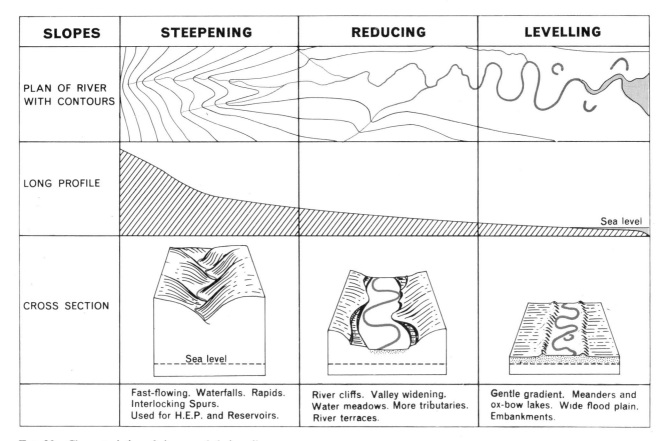

SLOPES	STEEPENING	REDUCING	LEVELLING
PLAN OF RIVER WITH CONTOURS			
LONG PROFILE			Sea level
CROSS SECTION	Sea level		
	Fast-flowing. Waterfalls. Rapids. Interlocking Spurs. Used for H.E.P. and Reservoirs.	River cliffs. Valley widening. Water meadows. More tributaries. River terraces.	Gentle gradient. Meanders and ox-bow lakes. Wide flood plain. Embankments.

Fig. 20 Characteristics of rivers and their valleys.

not all rivers exhibit the three stages of development. Some, like many mountain streams, are entirely Youthful whereas others, such as the Trent and the rivers emptying into the Wash have no Youthful Stage at all. See Map II, Fenland.

Glaciated Highlands

Many of the valleys of the Lake District, North Wales and Scotland and other mountainous regions cannot be explained by the work of rivers that flow through them today. They have been caused by the erosion of the valley glaciers which occupied them during the Ice Age. The sides of the valley are steep and the former **spurs truncated**; the valley floor is broad and contains a **mis-fit river**; the V-shaped river valley has become a **U-shaped glaciated valley.** Above the valley sides we may find **hanging valleys** leading back to armchair shaped hollows or **corries** (cwms) sometimes occupied by small lakes or **tarns.** When the corrie walls form narrow, angular ridges or edges they are called **arêtes** and they may converge in a single **summit or peak.** Excellent examples can be picked out on the Lake District map (Map 4), where the main valleys have been over-deepened and are occupied by lakes. The principal features of glaciated highlands are drawn on the block diagram and map—Figs. 21a and 21b.

Coastal Forms

The insular nature of the British Isles means that many of the Ordnance Survey Maps are coastal sheets and demonstrate a great variety of coastal scenery. The special Ordnance Survey symbols for **cliffs, sand, shingle** and **marsh** indicate the nature of the coastline. The lines on the map showing the Ordinary limits of High and Low Water reveal the width of the Shore Zone and the symbols for sand, mud and shingle indicate the **type of beach.** High tidal waters may extend well up river valleys, particularly in the **drowned estuaries or rias** of South-west England and South Wales and suggest thereby how far inland the river is navigable.

Fathom lines indicate the depth of off-shore waters; in deep water wind-driven waves attack outstanding **headlands** creating cliffs, small **peninsulas, caves, stacks** and natural arches and they drift the broken rock as sand and shingle into the shallower **bays** and along lowland coasts. At a river mouth or marked bend in the coastline this material might be drifted to form **shingle and sand spits** or bay-bars from headland to headland. Study these coastal forms on the maps of Looe and Aberystwyth (Maps 3 and 7). The more common features are illustrated in the map and diagram, Figs. 22a and 22b.

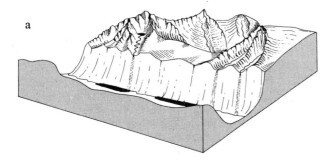

a

FIG. 21 (a) and (b).   Glaciated highlands.

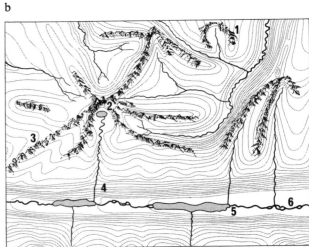

b

1. Corrie or cwm,
2. Corrie with tarn and pyramidal peak,
3. Arête,
4. Hanging valley waterfall,
5. Glacial lake,
6. Braided, misfit stream in 'U' shaped valley.

a

FIG. 22 (a) and (b).   Coastal forms.

b

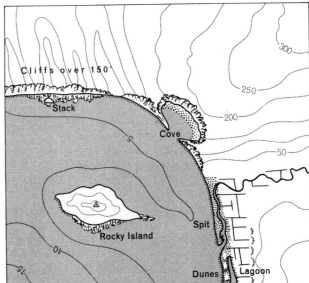

Chapter Five: The Identification of Rock-Types

The topographic map usually provides some indentifiable features that suggest the nature of the underlying rock. But lest the inexperienced map reader rushes in with hasty conclusions, where many experienced geographers and geologists fear to tread, a few words of warning must first be given. Quite commonly what appears as the clearest map evidence about rock type can be most misleading. On the Ingleborough map (Map 5) in this book the words ' Granite Quarries ' are written but the geologist would recognise the rock on field examination as arkose—a hard rock with the appearance and some of the properties of granite. No doubt it is quarried for road-building material and rough stone work, where granite might otherwise be used. Similarly ' Upper Slatepits ' (106319) on the Cotswolds map (Map 1) is no certain sign that slate is dug at this place; without any doubt it is not the grey or green slate that has been used extensively throughout the country as a roofing material, although it is possible that the rock in this part of the Cotswolds would split into thin slabs suitable for covering roofing timbers. Place-names unsupported by other evidence can lead to wrong conclusions, for instance, 'White Hill Farm' may have no connection with limestone outcrops; in reality, it may describe nothing more than lime-washed cottages. The term ' Downs ' is frequently used as evidence of chalk landscapes but this word occurs over a wide range of rocks to describe a range of low hills.

Nevertheless, by assembling different pieces of map evidence—the types of landform, the pattern of drainage, mineral workings, vegetation pattern, land use and place-names—we can often come to a tentative conclusion about the nature of the underlying rock strata. We should never make an assumption about the rocks on the basis of only one piece of evidence. Certainly the existence of quarries, clay-pits and brick-fields, lime-workings and cement works, etc., may well confirm one's deductions drawn from other facts. An elementary knowledge of the characteristics of common rocks and the landforms associated with them will often provide the most significant data in the interpretation of the physical landscape.

Some rocks are resistant to the forces of erosion and stand high in the landscape as mountains or hills; others are weak and more rapidly removed by the action of rivers, ice and the waves of the sea to form vales, valleys and bays. Where the rocks are broken by many joints and fissures and the rock minerals are soluble in the percolating ground-water, the drainage may quickly pass underground and the map will show a dry landscape with few surface streams. Such rocks are said to be *permeable*. On the other hand, where the map shows abundant surface streams, tributaries joining rivers, perhaps across ill-drained land, the rocks are largely *impermeable*.

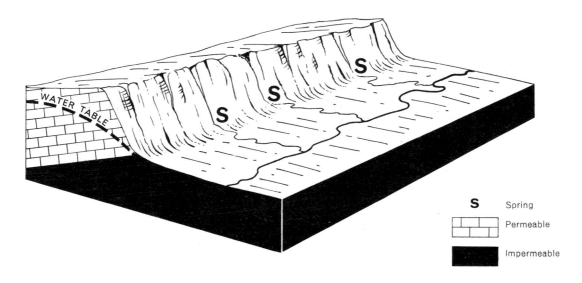

S   Spring

Permeable

Impermeable

FIG. 23   The Water table. At the junction of permeable and impermeable strata springs are usually found.

PLATE 1. SOUTH DOWNS NEAR LEWES

PLATE 1   The map and accompanying photograph show part of the South Downs escarpment near Lewes, Sussex.

The map and photograph should be compared and the following features noted:

The north facing scarp slope; hollows (coombes) cut into the scarp face; the plantation; the crest of the escarpment rising to Firle Beacon; the arable land in the vale (Vale of Sussex); the thin soil with chalk exposed in the quarries and scars.

The photograph shows the upper part of the back slope and this is continued on the map.   Numerous dry valleys can be seen, e.g. Tilton Bottom.

Suggest reasons for the small ponds, locations of farms, and pre-historic settlement.

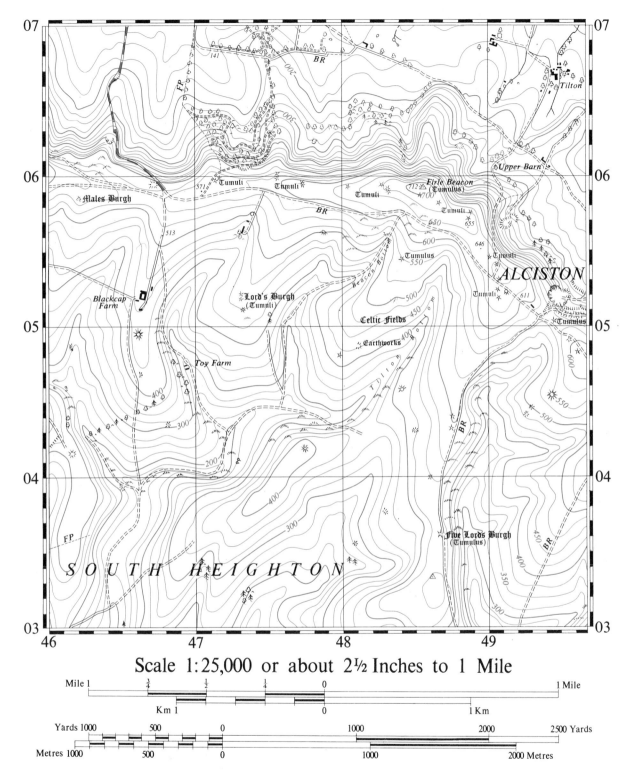

Scale 1:25,000 or about 2½ Inches to 1 Mile

FIG. 24   Map of the Chalk Downland near Lewes.

The Permeable Rocks

Rocks can be called permeable when, in humid regions there is little evidence of surface water, Their permeability may be due to a number of factors: to porosity—e.g. in some Sandstones; to solubility—e.g. in Limestones and those Sandstones held together by lime cement; and to the extent to which rocks are broken by systems of joints and fissures. All these factors may be working together in varying degrees. The underground water moves along joint planes and fissure lines to emerge at spring heads where relatively impermeable rocks outcrop, so that a line of springs indicates generally the junction between permeable and impermeable rock strata. Such a junction might reveal the division between major rock types—e.g. between clay and limestone or it might indicate simply a band of rock within the limestone or sandstone series. The upper limit of the underground water is called the water-table, and this is shown in Figure 23 in connection with the occurrence of springs.

Limestones

All rocks containing a high proportion of calcium carbonate are called limestones. In Britain the principal formations are:

(1) The crystalline limestones, largely of Carboniferous age which forms upland country, e.g. in the Craven District of the Yorkshire Pennines and in Derbyshire, the Mendips and parts of South Wales.

(2) The Jurassic limestones mainly oolitic in composition evident in the scarplands of the Midlands, the Cotswolds and the Hambleton Hills of north-east Yorkshire.

(3) The chalk, forming downland country in southern and eastern England.

The Carboniferous Limestone

This rock is highly permeable, the surface water disappearing below ground characteristically in small depressions known in England as 'pot-holes' or 'swallowholes'. The pot-holes are often given local names and can be identified at once on the map, e.g. Spice Gill Hole (736762) on the Ingleborough map (Map 5). In these regions the rock is strong enough to support caves in which the lime-charged waters deposit stalactites and stalagmites. The underground features cannot, of course, be portrayed on the map but because of their considerable interest to tourists they are frequently named on the map as: 'Caves', 'Passages', 'Water Swallows', etc. The higher slopes of the crystalline limestone may be broken by outcrops of bare rock, weathered into smooth blocks separated by shallow V-shaped depressions, the whole forming a fretted pavement of broken rock, called in Yorkshire clint and grike formation.

This broken ground is clearly seen on the photograph of Ingleborough Hill (Plate 5). A characteristic feature is the valley once containing water, but now dry, which may terminate abruptly in a pot-hole. Several pot-holes may occur at intervals along the dry valley floors be to filled only after a heavy storm. Occasionally dry gorges may be found, for example, at Cheddar in the Mendips, and at the Winnats Pass near Castleton in Derbyshire. When the features are widespread the term 'Karst' is applied to them, the name deriving from a large area of limestone scenery in north-west Yugoslavia.

In Part III of this book a detailed account of the limestones country around Ingleborough in the central Pennines will be found. This should be studied carefully and the exercises completed.

The Jurassic Limestones

These limestones form ranges of hills running from north Yorkshire through the Midlands to Portland Bill and exhibit a great variety of landforms, so that generalisation is very difficult. They form a typical escarpment in the Cotswolds, where the rocks have a moderate dip to the south-east. In north-east Yorkshire the angle of dip is much less so that the land form is that of a dissected plateau. More surface drainage is usually found in these regions than in chalk landscapes as the limestone may contain a fair proportion of clay and clay bands outcrop in some places. However, good examples of dry valleys can be found, particularly in the Cotswolds, though the complete dry valley systems of chalk regions are generally absent. The Cotswolds scarp face shows considerable dissection into hallows or coombes and we may find patches of woodland known locally as 'hangers' clinging to the upper slopes. Good examples are seen on the map extract of this region in Part III. (Map 1).

Bands of ironstone occur interbedded with the limestone and are of economic importance at Corby in Northamptonshire and Scunthorpe in Lincolnshire. In the Cleveland Hills of north Yorkshire the ironstone is now almost exhausted. The map should reveal these iron workings; using opencast methods they cover large areas.

The admixture of clay and limestone has produced a good soil in many regions of this type and settlements are more closely distributed than in the chalk and crystalline limestones regions. On the Lincolnshire Edge the land is used for arable farming right along the crest of the escarpment.

The Chalk

Although chalk is very permeable owing to its high porosity, the rock is mechanically weak and rarely support caves. Pot-holes are absent though occasional small 'sinks' may be noted on the map. This rock is the well known scarp-former of the North and South Downs and the Chilterns, the relatively steep scarp face often cut into coombes and the gentle back or dip slope dissected by dry valleys. Here the valley forms are complex with major valleys joined by many tributary valleys increasing in width down the back slope until the water-table appears at the surface. The valleys are steep-sided and their floors rounded as though by running water. After an unusual period of heavy rain the water-table may rise and rivers flow, albeit temporarily in these valley courses. Such temporary streams are called ' bournes ', ' winterbournes ' or lavants ', and the place-name ' bourne ' is found frequently in chalk regions. At the base or the scarp slope streams issue from springs and flows across the clay lands in vales.

The hills are generally lower than in the Carboniferous limestone regions and the rounded undulating outline of the chalk contrasts quite markedly with the angular sides and plateau summits of the harder limestone.

The natural vegetation of chalk lands is an open woodland of oak, hornbeam and beech with short turf, suitable for sheep grazing, but in recent years as farming techniques have changed, arable farming has extended over many former open pastures. A relic of the once extensive sheep farming on chalk and downland is the dew-pond. This is a small depression, either natural or man-made, lined with clay or floored with cement to collect rainwater for the watering of livestock. They are clearly distinguishable in blue on the one inch and 2½ inch maps

Today many are disused as the number of sheep has declined, and, in places thay have been replaced by cisterns drawing water from underground sources by means of pipes.

Other evidence that may help in confirming a diagnosis of chalk includes: the frequency of the use of the words ' Downs ' and ' Chalk ' in place-names; the occurance of white hill-figures ancient and modern; cement-works; and numerous antiquities, such as camps, tumuli and earthworks; for these more open areas were amongst the first settled by prehistoric man in Britain. But not one of these features by itself, should be considered of sufficient value to conclude that the land shown on any map is chalk country. A sketch-map of a typical chalk landscape of southern England is given in Figure 24; it has been drawn from a 2½ inch map of the South Downs near Lewes.

The Sandstones

Those sandstones rock that are cemented by lime or are loosely consolidated are frequently permeable, and dry valleys may be seen on the map. They occur chiefly in Lowland Britain (south and east of the Tees-Exe line) in the Greensand belts of the Weald of south-east England, at Sandringham, and in the glacial sands of the Breckland of Norfolk. The sandstone may form low ridges or ranges of hills, rising even to almost 1,000 feet above sea-level at Leith Hill in the Western Weald. Sands and sandstone for building purposes are much in demand and the O.S. symbol for sand pits can usually be found on the map. Further evidence is often forthcoming in the symbols used for vegetation. The

dry, acid soils of sandy regions support heath of gorse, broom and heather, and the O.S. maps distinguish the type of vegetation. Coniferous trees tolerate sandy habitats and in the lowland area if the tree symbols change from mixed or deciduous to coniferous woodland it is usually a good indication of a sandstone outcrop. Similarly, recent afforestation in lowland areas may be located on the poorer sandy soils, e.g. the Thetford and Brandon forests in Norfolk, and golf courses take advantage of the open undulating heaths. Finally, place-name evidence is almost certain to be seen in Sandpit Hill, Sand Gate Farm, the Sandlings, etc.

The Impermeable Rocks

Rocks are impermeable when they do not allow the free downward passage of water. This impermeability may be due to the closeness or absence of jointing which prevents the development of large open cracks in the rock, to the insoluble nature of the rock minerals or, as with clays, to the minute pore spaces that readily fill with water and prevent free circulation. Where these rocks outcrop at the surface, stream courses are everywhere evident and the land may be marshy and badly drained. Where the impermeable rocks outcrop below permeable strata they bring the water-table to the surface, and springs appear on the map. Impermeable rocks form both upland or lowland country.

The Clays

Many kinds of clay of various geological ages occur in Britain, and as weak rocks, easily worn down by the forces of weathering and erosion, they form open vales, e.g. the Jurassic clay plains of Oxfordshire and Bedfordshire, and the Gault Clay of the Vale of Holmesdale at the foot of the North Downs in Kent. Clay is highly porous but very impermeable, and the heavy soils that develop on this rock may require extensive drainage before cultivation is possible. Consequently map evidence will include straightened water-courses and artificial drainage cuts shown by thin blue lines.

Most of the major rivers of this country occupy these clay vales lying beyond the scarps of Lowland England. These rivers, for example, the Thames, Great Ouse and Trent, may be seen on the map flowing slowly across the vales in wide-sweeping meanders, collecting tributary drainage on their way to the sea. These clay regions were formerly forested with damp oak-woods, and here and there patches of deciduous woodland can still be seen.

In East Anglia, parts of Lincolnshire and east Yorkshire, boulder clay was dumped by the ice sheets of the last Ice Age and masks the underlying chalk. It gives rise to small dissected plateaus with perched water-tables and belts of trees amidst rich farmland that has been trenched with tile field drains and is today intensively cultivated.

Map evidence of numerous brickyards and clay pits is a sure sign of a clay outcrop; the old pits may be picked out, now filled with water as small ponds. Note that all badly-drained land does not signify an outcrop of clay rock for the O.S. marsh symbol by river banks and around the mouths of estuaries portrays the superficial alluvium deposited by the river.

The Sandstones

We have seen that some British sandstones are permeable but others are highly impermeable, such as the coarse Millstone Grit of the Pennines and the Pennant Sandstones of South Wales. These rocks are resistant and form wet, boggy moorland of heather, bilberry and cotton grass drained by innumerable streams locally named 'cloughs', 'gills' and 'becks'. In these regions surface water is abundant and the rainfall usually high so that open reservoirs can be constructed to supply with soft water, centres of population and industry often many miles away.

The sides of the moor will be cut into steep-sided valleys as the rivers flow swiftly to adjacent lowlands. Wherever a harder band of rock outcrops, small waterfalls and rapids will be seen.

The rock may provide excellent building material, particularly the flagstones of the Pennines, and numerous quarries attest the heavy demand for this rock in the construction of the long dry stone walls separating Pennine fields and the buildings of the industrial north of England.

In Scotland and part of south-west England the Old Red Sandstone has long resisted the attacks of running water, ice and wind, and stands boldly in the landscapes, rounded in general outline as mountain or plateau.

Igneous and Metamorphic Rocks

A very great variety of these rocks is seen in western Britain from Devon and Cornwall to Scotland. Generally, the rocks are very impermeable, particularly the metamorphic slates, and in these regions of heavy rainfall surface water is abundant. Landforms developed in these rocks show an infinite variety and include the frost-shattered gabbro pinnacles of the Black Cuillins in Skye, the rounded slate summits of Skiddaw in the Lake District and the granite plateaus of Dartmoor and Bodmin moor in south-west England. Some indication of rock-type may be gleaned from named quarries on the map and the Cornish granites are frequently associated with old mineral workings of veins of tin and arsenic and kaolin or china clay. But it would be foolhardy to attempt to draw conclusive evidence of these rock types solely from map evidence. Corroboration from a geological map would be essential.

In Part III the Lake District map (Map 4) shows mountains built of both igneous rock and slate; the Alloa sheet (Map 6) shows highlands formed of igneous rock material whilst slate underlies the area around Aberystwyth (Map 7) and much of the upland country about Looe (Map 3).

The Fenlands

Bordering the Wash of eastern England and in the lower course of the River Axe and neighbouring rivers in the West Country of Somerset are flat lands lying below the 50 foot contour. These regions were covered by water, both marine and fresh, when sea-level stood higher than it does to day. In the waters peat accumulated so that as sea-level fell there was revealed a broad expanse of marshland with fen vegetation of reeds and willows growing alongside the streams and rivers. The natural fenland was a waste of reed and water at the level of the general water-table, but for centuries the land has been reclaimed by an intricate system of drainage channels. Today a map of the fens shows a multiplicity of artificial drainage cuts. In eastern England the drains are integrated into a network of field drains flowing into dykes which in turn flow into main arterial drains or 'levels'. An excellent example of this type of country is seen in the map extract of the Middle Level of the Fens given in Part III (Map 2).

The principal characteristics that distinguish fenland from the marshland developed on clay rocks include the following: the overall level nature of the land; the low elevation, only a few feet above and occasionally even below sea-level; the long straight channels of the major drains embarked throughout their courses; the natural embankments of the rivers, often strengthened to prevent flooding, that have been built up above the general level of the shrinking cultivated fields; pumping stations to raise the water from one level to another; 'washes' of open pastures designed to take excess water in time of flood; a rectilinear pattern of roads leading to minor droves and following the drains, alongside which are isolated farms; and the frequent occurrence of the place-name 'fen'. On the small area of the one inch map extract referred to earlier, the word 'fen' appears six times. Villages are seen to be sited on slightly raised ground, small 'islands', that avoid the wet marshes.

In the Somerset fenland the word 'moor' is a misnomer, used to describe these lowlands. The correct word 'fen' is generally absent. Nor do we find in this smaller area the pattern of minor and major drains and pumping stations associated with the fenland around the Wash. Nevertheless the map should reveal the characteristic physical features of typical fenland. Other areas of fenland are to be seen in north Lincolnshire and across the Humber in Holderness.

Chapter Six: Types of Settlement

By the time of the Domesday Book record of 1086 it is clear that the general pattern of settlement in England had been established. The Anglo-Saxon and later Scandinavian settlement had brought the small, compact village to the English plain. Some villages decayed, and were lost for centuries, to be discovered only in recent years by the archaeologist and historian. But the majority survived; some grew into towns and even cities as geographical conditions changed; others, less favoured, remained as villages preserving even today the Anglo-Saxon grouping of farms and dwelling houses and the strip cultivation of the mediaeval open fields. Notable examples are the villages of Haxey, Lincolnshire, and Laxton, Nottingham. With the exception of a few settlements founded as industrial sites or holiday resorts all the villages and towns on the map put down their roots over one thousand years ago. These villages were seldom founded by chance. The immigrant and invader chose a site possessing natural advantages over surrounding locations. We should be able to find out from the map evidence the nature of these advantages, and give some reason why one site was chosen rather than another. In the course of time roads, and very much later, railways, linked most of these settlements so that a convergence of routes on all larger settlements is characteristic. We must remember that in this sense all towns are **nodal towns**, roads converging on a point, or node, but this is in consequence of the important position of the town and not the cause of it. It is true, however, that recent growth around an old-established site may be due to its command over road and rail routeways, as in the **gap towns** of Lincoln and Leeds and the **rail junctions** at Crewe and Swindon.

Rarely do we find that a village owes its location to simply one natural advantage but several geographical factors combine and we may distinguish in any settlement the factor of **site, situation** and **function.**

Site

This is the building site, the actual area of land on which the settlement stands. It may be flat and permit the easy construction of dwellings; it may be elevated above the floodplains of a river nearby and thus avoid the danger of flooding, yet have ready access to water supplies. The **shape** of the site is important, providing clues to the way in which the settlement has grown. Thus the shape may be **nucleated,** i.e. around a marked centre such as a village green, a market, a church or a castle; or it may have a **linear** shape as in a street-village.

Situation

The situation or position of the settlement is its relationship with surrounding land and water features. It is its geographical setting. We have seen in Chapter 5 how springs occur at the junction of permeable and impermeable rocks at the foot of the scarp slope of limestone hills and at the edge of a clay vale. This is a common situation for a **water-seeking settlement** but other advantages are usually also there. Thus the place avoids the wetter conditions of the clay vale and the steep slopes of the scarp face. Moreover the site may be sheltered from prevailing winds and in a favourable position for the exchange of goods produced in dissimilar geographical regions. The **fen-line villages** of Cambridgeshire occur around a spring-head below the scarp of the East Anglian Heights at the edge of the fen, where the fish, fowl and reeds of the fenland were exchanged for the farm produce of the upland.

Function

The principal function of a town may be immediately recognisable on the map from its situation and from name evidence—e.g. commercial ports, seaside holiday resorts, coal mining centres. But, apart from natural route-centre functions performed by most towns it may be difficult to say from the map evidence anything about a town's present activities, particularly since towns today fulfil several functions. Some of these would include; **Ports - commercial, fishing, ferry or packet stations; resorts and dormitory towns; mining and other centres of mineral extraction; centres of heavy industry and manufacturing towns and cities; market towns and centres of local government administration.**

Upland Settlements

In prehistoric and early historic times the lowlands of Britain were well-forested land or ill-drained marsh, so that Man's first routes were the ridgeways across the more open uplands. With a few exceptions where these trackways led to the coast or crossed a river valley all the earliest settlements were on **hill-tops**, along recognised trade routes and in commanding positions, providing defence from attack. The O.S. map shows clearly these antiquities in Old English style of printing as: 𝕮𝖊𝖑𝖙𝖎𝖈 𝕱𝖎𝖊𝖑𝖉𝖘; 𝕰𝖓𝖙𝖗𝖊𝖓𝖈𝖍𝖒𝖊𝖓𝖙𝖘; 𝕳𝖎𝖑𝖑 𝕱𝖔𝖗𝖙; 𝕿𝖚𝖒𝖚𝖑𝖎 (Burial Mounds). ' Celtic Fields ' indicates a site cultivated and settled for some time, but other sites may have been very temporary camps and defence-works.

Although some of these locations were later taken over and built on by Roman invaders and even by Norman Conquerors few have survived to the present day. Examples of prehistoric settlements now abandoned are Old Sarum near Salisbury, the British Camp on the Malvern Hills and Maiden Castle near Dorchester.

Roman settlements are shown in Roman capitals as: VILLA, CAMP, and the antiquities dating from A.D. 420 (when the Romans began to leave Britain) in Mediaeval type as: Castle, Manor, Moat. By the time of the Roman conquest settlements had spread to the valleys and vales as the woodland was slowly cleared. Upland settlement today includes **small nucleated villages** in sheltered positions around available water supplies, but few towns are seen. Alston in the northern Pennines of Cumberland, claiming to be the highest market town in England at 1,000 feet, has a population of only 2,300 (1960). For the rest, settlements are dispersed, the density of farms and other dwellings depending on the fertility of the soil, or the chance outcrop of rocks suitable for quarrying; or special factors such as Princetown on Dartmoor, supported by the prison.

Lowland Settlements

Man is essentially a lowlander and it is in the broad open vales and river valleys that our major towns and cities have grown. According to the principal geographical advantages of each one we can distinguish several types of settlement.

Dry-point Sites

On higher ground around marshes and along the floodplains of rivers, settlements avoided waterlogged conditions arising from the flooding of rivers at times of high tidal water and storm. The **fen-line village** of Lincolnshire, Cambridgeshire and Norfolk referred to above, and the **clay and gravel islands** rising above the level of the undrained Fens are on dry-point sites.

Examples

Downham Market (Map 2), Ely, March, Ramsey, Cheddar, Wells, and see also Figures 25a and 25b.

Wet-point Sites

Villages were founded around wells and springs where a pure and regular water supply was at hand. Such settlements are commonly found at the base of the scarp slope of limestone hills (see p. 41) strung out along a natural line at the spring-head. These are called **spring-line settlements.** They may also occur at the base of the dip or back slope.

Examples

At the base of Chalk escarpments of the South Downs, North Downs, Salisbury Plain, Lincoln Edge and the oolitic limestones of the Cotswolds and Northamptonshire uplands. See Figure 30,

Foot-hill Settlements

Villages have developed at the junction of lowland and upland where the hills afforded shelter from rough weather and the plain provided ease of communication. The settlements are frequently found where a river has cut through the hills giving access to higher ground. Spring-line settlements are also of this type.

Examples

The spring-line and fen-line settlements mentioned above; settlements in the Vale of Strathmore at foot of the Grampian Mountains and in the Vale of Pickering at the foothills of the North York Moors. See also Map VII and Figure 28.

Confluence Towns

Where two or three rivers meet and the valley routes converge we find the confluence town. It may also have a market function or operate as a river port.

Examples

Reading, Salisbury, Oxford, Tewkesbury and Monmouth. See Figure 26.

Market Towns

These are centrally situated in the areas they serve, their advantages of position causing them to grow at the expense of surrounding settlements. Because of their greater importance, roads and railways converge on them, emphasising their nodal situations.

Examples

Figure 27, Melton Mowbray; Bedford; Taunton; Hereford, and most other county towns.

Gap Towns

Road and railways converge to pass through a natural gap, usually cut by a river in a range of hills, thus providing the easiest route across the upland. A settlement in the gap will benefit from the traffic passing through it and many towns of this type can be found throughout the British Isles. Close examination of the gap may reveal the ancient nucleus around a castle or old fortification overlooking the gap, as at Lewes, Arundel and Lincoln. We should remember that the early importance of the gaps was due not to the routes through the valleys but to the ridgeways which were compelled to descend the valley slopes at these places.

Examples

Figure 29, Goring-on-Thames; the towns controlling routes through the North and South Downs and the Chilterns where paired gap towns may be found at the foot of both scarp and dip slopes, e.g. Leatherhead and Dorking; Princes Risborough and High Wycombe. Others include Hexham (Tyne Gap); Skipton (Aire

Continued on page 34

Fen Island Settlements

Early settlement in the lowlands around the Wash was made on small island sites above the surrounding marsh. These dry places provided a firm foundation for building and a refuge from flooding. Today the marsh has been drained and road and rail link the former islands to the neighbouring uplands. Haddenham, Wilburton and Sutton occupy low ridges between 50 feet and 100 feet and the surrounding fen in this area is near and in places below sea-level. The map shows that no new settlements have grown in the drained fen as the drying out has caused the peaty fen soil to shrink and this limits the construction of permanent dwellings. Thus the older island sites retain a greater importance as the only major settlements in the area.

Other examples of this type of settlement can be seen in the Levels of Somerset, formerly marshland which was drained about the same time as the Fens of eastern England, mainly under the direction of the same engineer, the Dutchman Cornelius Vermuyden. Island sites such as Glastonbury compare closely with Ely and the surrounding lowland shows similar features to the Fens with the straightened courses of the rivers Axe, Brue and Parrett and the dense network of field drains locally known as rhynes.

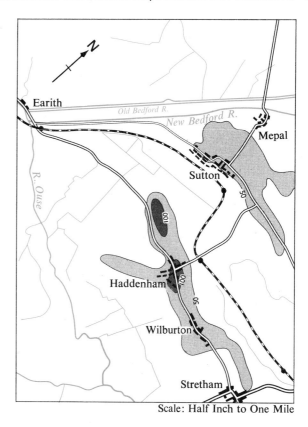

Fig. 25   (a) Fen island settlement.

Fen-line Settlement

The villages of Swaffham Prior, Swaffham Bulbeck and Burwell are representative of many settlements located at the junction of the fen and the upland. They occupy sites about 50 feet above sea-level and are raised slightly above the old marsh. These are the fen-line settlements. The sites are both water-shunning and water-seeking in that they avoid the damp fen, yet are located near fresh water springs. Many of these villages were formerly small fen ports used by barges of shallow draught transporting the fish, reeds and wildfowl of the fen to exchange for the corn and meat of the uplands. Through the intricate waterways of the region they were connected to the larger sea ports of the Wash.

A close study of parish boundary lines in the fen edge will usually show long narrow parishes running from the upland to the marsh. Within each parish the medieval villagers achieved some degree of self-sufficiency, summer grazing in the fen, good arable land at the scarp foot, a little timber from the hanger woods on the steeper slopes and building material by easy quarrying.

These maps jointly show a strip of country stretching to the north-west from the East Anglian Heights near Cambridge into the Middle Levels of the Fens. Compare with Map 1.

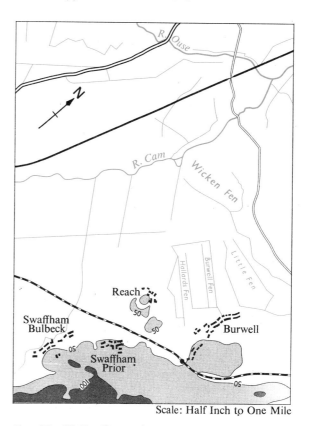

Fig. 25   (b) Fen-line settlement.

Gap); Stirling and Perth (in gaps cut by the rivers Forth and Tay between the Sidlaws, Ochils and Campsie Fells).

Bridge Towns

Wherever routes could cross a river or stream by a ford in early times and later by a bridge, the crossing-point often became the site of a settlement controlling the traffic. Not all bridge points attracted permanent settlement but particularly important was the lowest crossing point on a river, below which the tidal waters of the estuary were too wide and turbulent for bridge construction.

Examples

Figure 30, Bridgwater; Alloa (Map VI); London; Lancaster; Stirling and Perth; Gloucester.

Industrial Towns

The size of the larger towns and cities is generally dependent on their industrial activities but these are not always evident on the map. We can only suggest reasons for the earliest settlement and not for later growth. An example of one of the few towns growing around a single industry is at Skinningrove, north-east Yorkshire (see Map VIII).

Coastal Settlements

The insular nature and long indented coastline of the British Isles have provided many advantageous sites for settlements. They fall into two groups—the ports and the resorts.

The Ports

Commercial ports dealing in a great variety of trade and handling passenger traffic from the sea highways of the world have developed in deep sheltered estuaries away from the storms of the open sea. How far the deep water estuary has influenced the building of the ports may be judged from the lines on the map showing the extent of High and Low Water. The larger ports will show a long waterfront site backed by warehouses, dry docks, shipbuilding yards, offices, refineries and factories and behind them are sited the shops and residential suburbs. A few ports in similar situations have specialised as **naval dockyards**, building and servicing the Royal Navy. As ships have grown in size and the heads of some estuaries have become choked with silt **outports** have been constructed near the mouths of certain estuaries to deal with the vessels of larger draught. Although most ports will have a small fleet, fishing inshore waters, the principal fleets of deep-sea fishing vessels come from specialised ports with large fish markets, freezing and canning industries, and good rail facilities for quick despatch to urban markets. Grimsby, the second largest **fishing port** in Britain, is highly specialised, dealing almost exclusively in fish.

Facing the North Sea it is situated well down the Humber estuary. Of the smaller ports only a few retain any importance for fishing, e.g. Newlyn (Cornwall), Milford Haven (South Wales) and Whitby (Yorkshire).

Ferry ports or packet stations to the Continent, Ireland and the islands around our shores will show small dock factories, sufficient to cater for passenger embarkation and to deal with mail. They have grown up at a river mouth or on a headland with good rail connections to the major cities inland.

Examples

Commercial and Passenger Ports. London; Liverpool; Glasgow; Southampton; Hull; Newcastle; Bristol; Belfast.

Outports. Avonmouth; Tilbury; Cobh (for Cork).

Naval Bases. Portsmouth; Plymouth; Portland; Scapa Flow; Rosyth.

Fishing Ports. Grimsby; Fleetwood; Aberdeen; Hull; Lowestoft.

Ferry Ports. Dover; Folkstone; Newhaven; Tilbury; Harwich; Fishguard; Holyhead; Heysham; Weymouth; Stranraer and many other small ports serving the Scottish islands, e.g. Oban for Mull and Kyle of Lochalsh for Skye.

The Resorts

Holiday resorts, retiring-places and **dormitory towns** are to be seen in great numbers along many stretches of the coast. Their present-day function may have largely replaced an older fishing or trading port—at Hastings, Southend and Yarmouth—as the tourist industry has expanded. The characteristic site shows ribbon development above the cliffs or along the promenades. Advantages of situation may include some or all of the following factors: a wide sea-shore with sand or shingle beach; southerly aspect; shelter from prevailing winds; variety of scenery on the coast and immediately inland; proximity to large centres of population. The map evidence will include a large residential area, well laid-out parks, swimming-pools, a golf-course, etc.

Examples

Aberystwyth (Map 7), and many others should at once come to mind.

A few inland spas perform a similar function. Bath dates from Roman times but the other spas chiefly owe their importance to the eighteenth century habit of 'taking the waters', e.g. at Tunbridge Wells, Leamington Spa, Cheltenham, Harrogate and Buxton.

Confluence Town, Monmouth

This old county town is an example of the combination of several factors of site and situation.

(a) Confluence between the river Wye and its tributary, the Monnow, providing a small area of land suitable for building.

(b) Gap town and route centre where three valley ways and two ridgeways converge.

(c) Defence site encompassed on three sides by water and high ground to the north. Monmouth was one of the most important towns along the Welsh Marches guarding the route to the west.

(d) Market centre served by major and minor roads and, until recently, by three branch line railways.

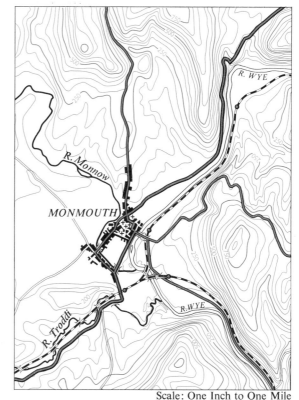

Scale: One Inch to One Mile

FIG. 26   Confluence town, Monmouth.

Market Town, Melton Mowbray

Centrally situated in the rich dairy farming area of the Wreake Valley, Melton Mowbray is the focus of numerous roads and the crossing place of two main line railways. The east-west line, the old Midland and Great Northern, is now closed to passengers. The traditional market in butter, cheese, meat and other agricultural produce is today supplemented by food manufacturing industries and by some heavy industry on the Leicester iron-ore field. Many market towns have wide, high streets and squares with centrally situated corn exchanges, butter markets and wool halls. The detail of the larger scale maps should show this plan, a wide central area with public buildings in black.

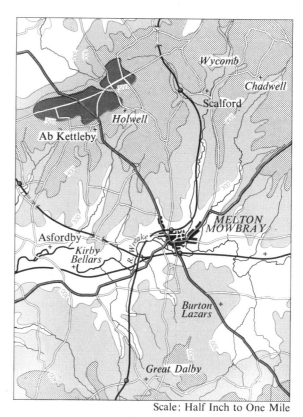

Scale: Half Inch to One Mile

FIG. 27   Market town, Melton Mowbray.

Foot-hill Settlement, Alva

The small town of Alva is situated at the foot of the
Ochil Hills. The site lies above the flood plain of the
River Devon between the 50 feet and 150 feet contours
on a small platform where a tributary stream—the
Alva Burn—leaves its restricted upland valley and
enters the broader main valley. At the junction of
upland and lowland the speed of the burn has been
checked and Alva is probably sited on alluvium dropped
there by the stream. The fast flowing stream provided
power and soft water for a small wool industry, using
the local clip.

Compare with Map 6 and Plate 6 in Chapter 14.

Scale: One Inch to One Mile

FIG. 28 Foot-hill settlement, Alva.

Gap Town, Goring-on-Thames

In the narrow gap cut by the Thames between the
Chilterns and Berkshire Downs, Goring and Pang-
bourne control the road and rail routes which link the
London Basin in the south with the Oxford Clay Vale
to the north. The through valley of the Thames is the
only lowland gap in this part of the chalk escarpment.
Other routeways crossing the Chilterns make use of
cols and must cross the scarp slope into the northern
vale. The map shows two locks on the river Thames
indicating that here there is a navigable waterway
although somewhat shallow. Traffic is confined to
small barges and pleasure craft and Goring, therefore,
shares in this trade.

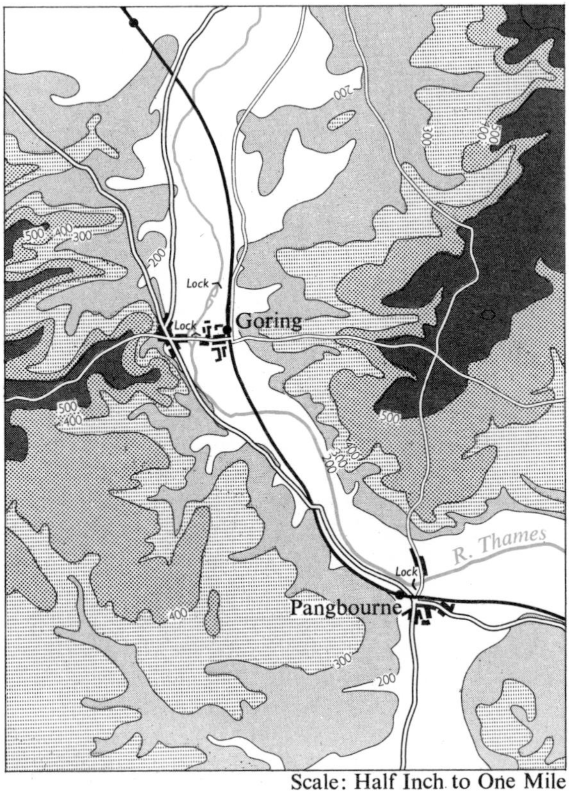

Scale: Half Inch to One Mile

FIG. 29 Gap town, Goring-on-Thames.

Spring-line Settlement, Wiltshire

Spring-line settlement. Wiltshire. The villages of Cliffe Pypard, Compton Bassett, Cherhill, Blackland, and Calstone Wellington lie on or near the spring-line about 400 feet above sea-level at the foot of the scarp of the Marlborough Downs. Compare these sites with those shown on Figure 25b. Other than the supply of fresh water there were probably several other advantages of both site and situation. The position is sheltered in a dissected scarp face and at the break of slope building would not be too difficult and mixed soils offered some prospect for agriculture. This area of England saw some of the first farming by Neolithic peoples on the easily cleared higher slopes of the chalk upland. Later early Medieval settlement spread to the present scarp foot sites.

Settlements in a similar position can be seen at the base of the limestone escarpment of the Cotswolds (Map 1).

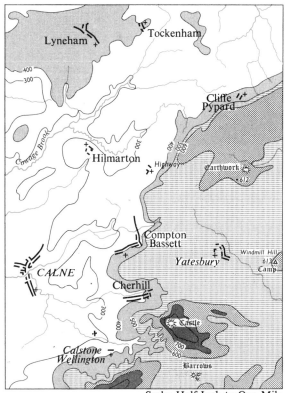

Scale: Half Inch to One Mile

Fɪɢ. 30 Spring-line settlement, Wiltshire.

Bridge Town, Bridgwater

Bridgwater in Somerset has grown up at a convenient crossing point on the River Parrett. Below the town the river was too wide for easy bridge construction so that coastal roads must turn inland to cross the river near the head of its estuary. Highbridge, on the River Brue, to the north, is another example of settlement located at the lowest bridging point. Both town have the further advantage of being situated at the head of navigation of the rivers on which they stand. Other examples can be found well inland from the coast. Place name evidence for the origin of the settlement may often be seen as in ' Cambridge ' and ' Oxford '.

Today these old bridge town are losing some of their importance as traffic is diverted to more direct routes over wide estuaries, such as the Forth, Severn and Tay. These new bridges carry modern highways and are unlikely to attract settlement of any kind.

Scale: Half Inch to One Mile

Fɪɢ. 31 Bridge Town, Bridgwater.

Chapter Seven: Communications

We can imagine Man in the early civilisations of the Middle East drawing in the soil or sand and making the first maps. They would be route-maps, recording journeys and fixing important landmarks, and would be transferred later to stone tablets or papyrus. So, as the civilised world expanded the new cartographers would fill in details on maps and charts of these new routes overland and across the seas. In Britain the Romans produced itineraries, setting out distances along the great roads they built, and in the seventeenth century, a well known map-maker, John Ogilvie, constructed elaborate road-strip maps similar to those issued today by the motoring associations. But these were not maps in the true sense, as they simply recorded distances and paid little attention to scale; direction was largely ignored. On modern maps all forms of communications are shown and distances can be measured accurately in terms of the scale of the map.

Roads

The Ordnance Survey distinguish roads by their width and their surface. From the map symbols we can recognise fenced and unfenced roads, footpaths, trackways and the various roads classified by the Ministry of Transport, including the new Motorways.

Footpaths

These are found in open country and in the hills and mountains where construction of metalled road surfaces is unnecessary or impracticable. The prehistoric ridgeways can be distinguished from other footpaths and tracks by their accompanying tumuli and other antiquities. They are frequently named, e.g. the Icknield Way crossing the chalk downland of south-east Cambridgeshire. The military Roman roads can be seen by their straight stretches marching across the countryside, ignoring the contours, and by the ancient names of Watling Street, Ermine Street, Stane Street, etc.

The origin of the rolling English road probably can be found in the ' green roads ' and cattle droves of the Middle Ages. It can be identified picking its way across the lowlands of Britain linking up ancient settlements, skirting the old field boundaries and avoiding marshland and steeply rising ground. In great contrast are the roads of recent date. They have the straight course of the old Roman roads negotiating wet land and hill sides by embankments, cuttings and viaducts, to maintain a flat and level surface. Examples of the new roads should be sought on the relevant sheets of the O.S. maps—e.g. the improved sections of the A1, the Great North Road; the sections of Motorways, London-Birmingham; the Preston By-Pass, the Ross Spur (Hereford) and Birmingham-Preston.

Rivers

Rivers must have been used from the earliest times as a way into the interior from the coast. The extent to which they are used today for communications cannot always be discovered from the map. The location of various types of ports near the river mouth has been discussed in Chapter 6 (p. 34), but further upstream, even beyond tidal influence, the river may act as a highway for small craft, such as barges and other motor boats. The occurrence of locks, towing paths, piers for unloading, straightened courses, dense building near the riverside will suggest this kind of use. The river Trent carries a considerable traffic as far inland as the Potteries. Although road and rail transport have taken away much of the river cargo some river ports are still important. They include Wisbech on the Nen, and Norwich on the river Wensum.

Canals

The majority of canals were dug in the eighteenth century to carry the bulk goods of the Industrial Revolution. We should expect to see them linking the old centres of heavy industry joining the navigable sections of rivers and leading to London and the seaports. Although much of this trade was quickly taken over by the railways, and many are today unused, they are immediately recognisable on a map. Note how, unlike rivers, they maintain long straight sections along the contours, moving from one level to another by means of locks. The coal-field centres of industry are found on the edge of the uplands and so great engineering skill was called for in the cutting of the canals. In the Midlands of England, across the Pennines between Yorkshire and Lancashire, and on the Welsh border the map reveals the work of the canal builders—in the construction of aqueducts, embankments and locks, and in the digging of cuttings and canal tunnels. There should be no confusion between the waterways and rivers as seen on the map: the canals are named in blue, Grand Union Canal, Aire and Calder Canal, etc., and a towing path for the horse-drawn barge runs alongside. Drainage channels which also follow a straight course are distinctively named, e.g. Middle Level Drain in the Fens (Map 2).

Railways

The nineteenth century was the great period of railway construction. Only in the very remote parts of Britain could one find a map with no section of railway track; in just over a hundred years the railways were extended the length and breadth of the land. Like canal construction, railway construction was also controlled by relief. The lines seek out the river gaps and passes and maintain a level course by cuttings, bridges, viaducts and embankments. Where gradients were too steep for cuttings to be made tunnels were dug. The long tunnels across the Pennines—The Summit, Standedge and Woodhead tunnels—demonstrate how physical barriers were overcome.

On the O.S. map we can distinguish, by the symbols, between multiple and single tracks, small gauge and mineral working lines, and all the constructional detail is given alongside the track. These railways followd as direct a course as relief and land purchase permitted, joining up the larger centre of population, so that villages in non-industrial areas were often by-passed or the station built a short distance away. Today the greater volume of road traffic has compelled the railways to close unprofitable branch lines, many small stations, and halts. The closed station is indicated by an open circle across the line. Many places were stimulated in their growth by the arrival of the railway and a few owe their present importance almost entirely to it. Crewe, Rugby, Swindon and Eastleigh are large junctions where the repair and manufacture of railway engines and rolling stock is carried out. The small town of Wolverton in Buckinghamshire was almost completely created as a wagon and repair centre.

Air Communications

Because of the long runways required and the undesirable noise and danger of modern aircraft, airfields are at some distance away from the heavily built-up areas they serve. Thus the airports for London are many miles away from the city's centre at Heathrow, Gatwick and Southend. Aerodromes acting as passenger terminals are named on the map as 'Airports' and runways may be shown by broken lines; others for military and club use are simply marked 'Airfield.'

Description of a Route

Examination questions on the subject of communications are generally of two kinds: (1) a description of a route along a footpath, river, road or railway; (2) the relationship between communications and the land and water features.

(1) Route description should keep to the area crossed by road, rail, etc., and the features close by. Do not describe distant prospects, but indicate the course taken by reference to distance, direction, elevation, slope, nature of land forms crossed; and to the surface and special features of construction, such as tunnels and level crossings, road junctions and bridges. An example of such a description is given below, taken from the Aberystwyth map (Map 7)—Llangorwen Church (603838), to Caeffynnon (588804).

' The B4572 leaves Llangorwen in a southerly direction crossing the Afon Clarach through a small patch of mixed woodland. For the next quarter mile it rises gently towards the steep valley slope. At the 125 foot contour the road rises following a zig-zag course, through the steep, wooded slope for about a half-mile. A trackway from the north-east joins the road at the shoulder (604829) and it then climbs over the summit of the plateau to meet the major road into Aberystwyth. The descent to this town is gradual, the road dropping from 350 feet to near sea-level in about one mile. It passes through the most heavily built-up area of the town and crosses the Rheidol by the bridge (583813). To the south the road runs along a coastal flat for just over 200 yards at Trefechan. The road passes below the railway and makes a sharp bend eastwards to avoid the steep slopes of Pendinas. As the A 487 it runs to the south-east about 100 feet above sea-level to the new housing estate at Caeffynnon.'

(2) Relationship to relief and drainage. This type of question seeks information about the ways by which roads, railways and canals avoid steep gradients and the wet valley bottoms; how they approach bridging-points across a river, and negotiate hill ranges through gaps and passes.

We can now examine the same route on the Aberystwyth map described above to illustrate the difference in the two approaches to route description, this time relating the road to the relief and drainage.

' Leaving the church the road crosses by means of a small bridge (603838) the Afon Clarach approaching directly the lower slopes of the valley. At G.R. 602835 it begins to climb the steep north slope of the upland and to reduce the gradient it crosses the slope obliquely and doubles back to reach the summit. The road then crosses the broad watershed without difficulty and descends to Aberystwyth, avoiding a narrow valley floor and small stream in Grid Square 5982. Through the town centre the relief is low and flat; the road turns south seeking a bridge point over the Rheidol at G.R. 583813. To the south of Trefechan it turns abruptly eastwards to pass around the flanks of Pendinas Hill and well above the flood plain of the river.'

Other examples of this kind of control are given in the map analyses in Part III. Note particularly the analysis of the Alloa sheet (Map 6).

Chapter Eight: Land Use

How much can we discover from the map of the many different ways in which the earth's surface is used by Man? There is the direct evidence of actual buildings, a clear form of land use; and by names and symbols we can see other uses, such as mines, quarries, reservoirs, parkland, orchards and other semi-permanent features. But the farming use of land is not so permanent, changing as management and market conditions change, and so no indication of the type of farming is given. Special Land Use maps on a scale of 1 : 63,360 were published before the war, but these have now little more than historical interest. A new series of maps is being published on the 1 : 25,000 scale in the Second Land Utilisation Survey of Britain, directed by Alice Coleman, M.A., and at the present time (1970) 100 sheets are available. The information about land use is overprinted in colours on the O.S. topographical map and each sheet corresponds exactly to two sheets of the Ordnance map. From the standard topographic map our interpretation of farming activities will be inferred from the nature of the land surface and its drainage, the density of farms and any special symbols employed.

Farming Land Use

A high density of farms indicates a high fertility of soil and intensive farming. The close network of drains in the Fens (Map II) implies a rich soil yielding a high return to offset some of the heavy costs of drainage. Whether arable crops or pasture predominate cannot be told, but a knowledge of the economic geography of the country will enable us to make a calculated guess. Land under orchards is shown by a regularly spaced tree symbol and horticulture by a glasshouse device. In upland areas a rough grazing symbol is used on uncultivated land and we can safely conclude that the occasional farms rear flocks of sheep. Similarly, lowland marshes are more likely to be used for cattle grazing rather than for cultivation, although Romney Marsh is traditionally a sheep grazing area.

Woodland

A distinction is drawn between coniferous, deciduous and mixed woodland by pictorial symbols. Afforested areas can usually be spotted as they are almost entirely of conifers and the boundary enclosures are more regular than those around natural forests and woods.

Mineral Extraction

The quarry symbol locates the extraction of rocks such as building stone, ironstones, limestone and chalk; the open pit symbol indicates the loose diggings of sand and gravel. Underground extraction is seen by the word 'Mines', and this will usually mean coalmines today.

Industrial Use

We must look for the functional arrangement of buildings around railway-sidings, quays, and some named evidence of industry, e.g. factory, mills, works, docks. The nature of the work is not given. From the shape of the buildings and such features as the small circles representing oil storage tanks and gas-holders, the presence of industry can be deduced.

Recreational Use

In and around large centres of population and at the seaside, will be found parks, gardens, playing fields, golf courses, etc. In areas of great natural beauty we shall find the National Parks, Nature Reserves and National Trust Properties, and alongside stretches of water, such as the Norfolk Broads, we can expect to see mentioned the Sailing Club Houses and attendant boat and mooring yards.

Waste Land

This can usually be inferred in areas of very high, badly drained land and on surfaces of broken rock such as the high mountains and moorlands of Britain. Similarly coastal dunes, mudflats and saltmarshes have very low economic value. Tip heaps and spoil heaps, the by-products of mining and heavy ore refining fall into this category although disused quarries may have some value for the dumping of public refuse.

Examples

Consult the relevant map-extracts.
Farming. Contrast Maps 1 and 2 with Maps 4 and 5.
Woodland. Map 4—note distribution of natural woodland and afforestation.
Mineral Extraction and Industry. Maps 6 and 8.
Recreational. Compare evidence on Maps 4 and 7.
Waste Lands. Exposed and rock-strewn ground— Maps 4 and 8.

The map-extract of Sheet 144 of the one inch O.S. map shows part of the Cotswold scarp and the adjacent Vale of Evesham. Many of the features outlined in Chapter 4 are well represented. Examine Figures 18a and 18b and 19a showing the origin of scarp and vale topography and then compare it with the block diagram, Figure 32, and the map. Let us now apply our knowledge to the most significant features shown on the map.

Relief

At the outset distinguish between Relief and Elevation. Relief here (from base of scarp slope to crest of escarpment) is roughly 700 feet, and from the lowest part of the vale to the crest the maximum relief is over 900 feet. The escarpment rises to an elevation of 1,048 feet, which is very high for British scarplands.

The scarp face trends approximately north-north-east to south-south-west and has been deeply dissected by small streams, producing an indented or fretted scarp. The dissection has reached an advanced stage. A small hill detached from the main escarpment exhibits a similar form to the main upland, and it appears that this knoll may have been isolated by the backward erosion of the river Isbourne and a neighbouring stream, which leaves the map south of Alderton. If this is so, the term outlier should be given to the knoll.

Drainage
The Uplands

The general absence of surface drainage is at once evident. The streams flowing down the scarp slope rise at approximately 700 feet but on the back slope only one stream appears, draining south through the valley of Cutsdean (088302). Careful examination shows other valley forms indicated by the contours, e.g. the valley containing Hornsleas Farm (123322). This is a good example of a dry valley. This evidence points to a permeable rock strata. Similar waterless features are exhibited by the knoll near Dumbleton, providing further information towards confirming its origin as an outlier.

The Lowlands

With their numerous watercourses the lowlands provide a great contrast to the uplands. The major stream of the area is the river Isbourne flowing north which is joined by many tributaries on its right bank. The presence of so much surface water indicates impermeable rocks.

Settlement
The Uplands

No large settlements can be found; Snowshill (0933) and Cutsdean (0830) are obviously small villages, each with a parish church. The remaining habitations are isolated farms, e.g. Peter's Farm (121363) and Springhill House (127340). There is much evidence of ancient occupation of these uplands in Tumuli and Barrows (burial chambers), at (117383) and a hill-fort 'Camp' at (080335).

The Lowlands

The settlements mainly nucleated in villages, include the following types:
(a) scarp-foot villages, e.g. Stanway, Stanton and Buckland. Dumbleton and Broadway are situated in similar positions; the former at the base of the outlier and the latter, a street village, at the break of slope between the vale and the uplands. All these are dry sites avoiding the damp lowland where early building was possible and drinking water nearby. Note that the actual spring-line appears to be above the general height of the villages.
(b) river and stream sites, e.g. Aston Somerville, Toddington and Sedgeberrow, located within short distances from streams but slightly above the river bank.
(c) scattered farms.

Communications
Roads and Trackways

The upland area has a high density of footpaths and tracks, fenced and unfenced minor roads; the A44 road through Broadway and the B4077 are the only examples of Ministry of Transport roads Classes 1 and 2. The large number of trackways indicates a close network of communications from early times and is characteristic of the drier upland areas in Britain. The existence of so few major roads in this part of the map is probably due to the absence of large settlements and the engineering difficulties in constructing modern highways in this kind of terrain.

On the other hand, in the lowlands major roads are more in evidence with longer straight stretches and footpaths and tracks are largely missing. It is significant that the major roads here do not pass directly through the small settlements and probably link larger towns beyond the limits of the map-extract.

Railways

Three stretches of main line railway are to be seen, which avoid the greater undulations of the scarp foot, and the wetter areas of the river valleys. With the exception of a tunnel (0130) the construction of the railway appears to have presented few problems.

No other signs of communications can be found.

Land Use

The widespread presence of large farms over the entire map, and orchards in the lowlands, and the absence of much rough grazing and woodland suggests that farming is the principal land use. Patches of mixed woodland are found mainly on the steeper slopes. In addition there are several large parks, probably country estates.

Only one quarry is shown (078302) and we can assume that mineral extraction is almost non-existent in this area. Nor is there any sign of industry.

Summary

We can now make some tentative conclusions, from this interpretation, about the nature of this scarpland area. The permeability of the upland is in little doubt, suggesting limestone or sandstone rocks but confirmation of a more positive kind (e.g., named quarries, etc.) is lacking. The smooth outline of the relief and the prominent dry valleys remove the possibility of Carboniferous Limestone, and the presence of many deciduous trees and the numerous settlements suggests a richer soil than is usually found on upland sandstones. Map evidence, by itself, is not enough to prove chalk or Jurassic limestone but the student should know that chalk escarpments in Britain do not reach an elevation of more than 1,000 feet.

As shown in Chapter 5, the most likely rock-former of impermeable lowland is clay but the conclusive evidence in form of clay-pits, etc., cannot be found on the map.

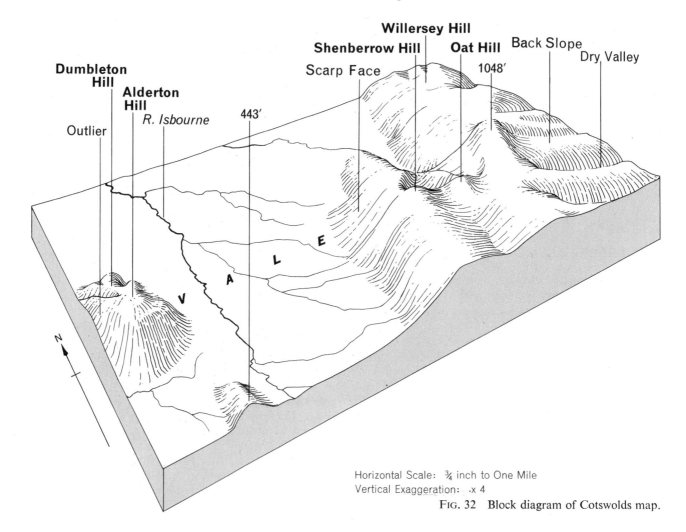

Horizontal Scale: ¾ inch to One Mile
Vertical Exaggeration: .x 4

FIG. 32 Block diagram of Cotswolds map.

Chapter Ten: Fenland: The Middle Level Map 2

The map extract shows a very typical piece of the English Fens and a small portion of the bordering upland. One of the four major rivers of the Fens, the Great Ouse, and several main drains appear on the map.

Relief

The upland area in the east, although small, is clearly a separate region and could well be divided from the rest of the map by the 50 foot contour line or the railway line could conveniently be used. The rest of the map is a well-drained lowland and heights nowhere exceed 50 feet; indeed, very careful examination shows several spot heights only just above sea-level—at 568100, 587095, and 555053 the land is actually at sea-level.

Drainage

Of all the water courses on the map only that of the River Ouse appears natural, winding between the embankments that show little straightening by man. The other water courses clearly show man's influence either in part, or along the entire straight course of the drains. Several types of drain are shown:

   i. Field drains that are, in fact, ditches around individual fields.

   ii. Larger connecting drains, e.g. Chancellor's Dike into which the field drains flow, and

   iii. The main level drains, e.g. the section of the Middle Level Main Drain.

All the main drains are embanked, indicating a high water level. Careful examination of the map will reveal spot heights at or near sea-level very close to these drains and this suggests that the river level is above that of the surrounding fields. At Denver, 587010, several important features of the drainage should be noted: the two major drains joining the Ouse above the Sluice Gate on the river; the controlling locks on the western drain; and to the east of the river a drain unconnected to the main system suggesting a new cut under construction.

Settlement

The principal settlements are the villages and one small town, Downham Market.

The Villages

Villages are indicated on the one inch map by the Ordnance Survey use of a characteristic style of printing as seen in the name 'Outwell' (5104). At Outwell and Upwell we see typical street-type villages, the buildings strung out along both sides of the road. This settlement plan is seen along the two main roads entering Outwell from the south-west and south-east. On a smaller scale, Nordelph and Emneth Hungate show the same form. Away from these villages buildings follow the roads and droves as in the 'ribbon development' along Barroway Drove.

The other villages in the east are along a marked natural line from Denver through Wimbotsham to Stow Bardolph. This line marks the edge of the drained lowland and coincides approximately with the 50 foot contour. There is some evidence to suggest a spring line at this height as tiny streams emerge near the villages and flow to join the Ouse. Each village is nucleated around a cross-roads and is linked by the major road, the A10, which seeks to avoid both the upland and the wetter lowlands.

Runcton Holme is the remaining village to be dealt with and this actually lies on the lowland. There is insufficient evidence to account for its origin.

Downham Market

This small town is also situated on the same natural line, but has outgrown its neighbours. The map does not suggest clearly the causes of this growth except that it is a focus of main roads, but the railway station is three-quarters of a mile outside the town and the River Ouse a mile due west shows no sign of a river port.

Dispersed Settlements

The absence of large parkland estates so familiar in other parts of Britain could indicate both the recent occupation of the farmland and its high fertility. This is supported by the density of farms. The farms are evenly distributed, served by minor roads and trackways.

Communications

A Trunk Road runs north-south at the edge of the upland and lowland, linking small settlements. The twisting course, followed by the two other main roads, seems unnecessary in such flat country, but the map shows some reasons for this course, e.g. in Outwell the two parallel main roads follow the banks of a drain. The numerous minor roads and droves linking the scattered farms and cottages generally follow a straight course, often on the top of the dikes or embankments, e.g. Edge Bank, 5106.

The main railway follows a direct course, avoiding the central lowland and main river. The railway track from Upwell through Outwell could be a mineral line, a tramway or a siding. The last is the more likely for the fruit trains serving the orchards along this route.

In this kind of landscape traffic might be expected on the waterways and the width of the Ouse suggests it could well be used for river craft and the presence of a lock near Denver lends some support to this view.

Land Use

Woodland is entirely absent from the drained lowland and there is much evidence to confirm the impression of a very fertile soil. The high density of farm buildings and the roads serving them has been noted. The fields are small and the network of drains is such that it could only be maintained by a prosperous farming community.

As the general level of the land is close to sea-level, flooding of fields seems likely and we might expect pasture to be the principal land use. The land around Outwell and Upwell is under orchards and there is no evidence to indicate other forms of land use.

Industrial occupations are conspicuously absent from the map apart from the word 'Mills' near Downham Market, at 603030.

Summary

The place-name evidence of 'Fen' is sufficient by itself to fix the location of the map and the character of the lowland. With this knowledge we can turn to the supporting evidence of the drains and levels to see that this is one of the most intensively farmed areas in Britain. In fact, the drained land is mainly devoted to arable farming and market gardening. The settlements are found on small 'islands' raised slightly above fen level or along the fen edge, i.e. 'fen-line' villages.

Chapter Eleven: River Valleys and Coasts Map 3

The map extract covers a small part of the Cornish Coast and displays many of the typical features of this region. The East and West Looe Estuary is a miniature of the larger estuaries of the area and the settlement is characteristic of many small British ports.

Relief

An upland area of low elevation meeting the sea in high cliffs is dissected by the lower courses of the East and West Looe Rivers and by many small fast flowing streams. Cross-sections will show steep, convex sided valleys and rounded or plateau-like summits. (Note the contour interval is 25 feet and not 50 feet as on the one inch map.) One would expect the valleys to be broad with gently sloping sides near their mouths and evidence must be sought to explain their present form.

Drainage

Let us note at the outset the limits of Ordinary High Tides in the main valleys. The whole of the East Looe and most of the West Looe on the map is tidal; at low tide the rivers discharge into the sea along well-marked channels through mud banks that fill the lower courses. In grid square 2455 the East Looe is braided and the valley section of the West Looe shows marked meanders. These features are consistent with a river in old age depositing a heavy load of sediment, but the valleys containing the rivers show a more youthful form and the river courses flow between steep valley sides and not across a wide, open flood-plain. The tributary valleys have a prominent 'V' shape cross-section and a steep long profile, e.g. the river in grid square 2453, and in every way can be described as youthful. Several springs occur in the south-west of the area above the cliff-line, the water probably draining direct to the sea.

Coastal Features

An upland coast is represented with marked cliffs rising to over 100 feet and below them a narrow, rocky shore zone in places broad enough to be called a wave-cut platform, e.g. at Hannafore Point (grid square 2552). Offshore several small islands are probably the remains of a former headland, the largest being St. George's or Looe Island. The smaller islands just offshore are properly called stacks.

Very little beach is to be seen—a small beach, mainly sand, at East Looe and tiny pockets of shingle elsewhere.

Settlement

The twin settlements of East and West Looe form the only population centres of any size. East Looe appears to be the major settlement as it is the terminus of the railway and a small port. The evidence for this is seen in the small pier or mole with entrance beacon and the railway siding along the water's edge. The deep water channel hugs the East Looe side. The only beach of any size is found in the shelter of the mole. The size and shape of the town is very obviously controlled by the estuary mouth and the steep-sided valleys. Buildings have spread northwards along a narrow, low shelf and into a small tributary valley—Shutta.

West Looe faces across the estuary and the centre appears to be at a valley mouth from which buildings have spread northwards along the estuary and also westwards towards the head of the valley. The buildings at Hannafore appear modern and probably represent the new residential development facing the sea, with access to beaches and sheltered from westerly winds. See Figure 33.

The remaining settlements include a very small village at St. Martin with a parish church and several other very scattered hamlets and farms.

Communications

The one railway line is controlled by relief and closely follows the left bank of the East Looe River. For most of its length the track is embanked on the river side and the road runs close by, both sharing the narrow ledge of land just above water level. The road seeks a bridging point which lies north of the centres of the two settlements and has been built across almost the widest part of the lower estuary.

We might expect the bridge point to have been nearer the mouth where the present secondary road in East Looe meets the river bank. The two other principal Ministry of Transport Roads ascend the valley sides and cross the uplands, making no use of the small valley floors. Numerous tracks and footpaths and some minor roads link the upland settlements. The Landmarks, beacons and the mole at East Looe suggest inshore navigation. The presence of the old canal marked in the upper reach of the East Looe River suggests that this part of the river also can be used at least by barges.

Land Use

The largest fields are found on the flatter summits with small fields on the shoulders of the upland blocks and mixed woodland on the steepest lower slopes. Careful examination will show the symbol for orchards around most of the small settlements and farms. We have seen already that East Looe functions as a small port and there is sufficient map evidence to conclude that the coast around East and West Looe is used by holiday-makers. There are five quarries named on the map; it is impossible to say the nature and purpose of this mineral extraction.

Two mills can be seen in the West Looe Valley. Note that the lower mill, in West Looe, is located in the downstream corner of what appears to be a large pool. This is possibly a tidemill and the pool serves as a reservoir of tidal water. Only local knowledge would confirm this.

Summary

A dissected plateau is cut into wide open valleys through which flow slowly the two rivers, depositing mud in the estuary. Other features of old age are seen in the meandering course of the West Looe River and the braided section of the East Looe. Why should the rivers show features of old age in a landscape otherwise mature? A clue may be sought in the tributary valley in grid square 2555. The outfall of this river has been blocked by man forming a small reservoir; this has checked the river's flow causing it to deposit its load and marshland is to be seen. The Looe estuary has been similarly invaded by the sea and this is one of many drowned estuaries or rias of South-west England. The cliffed coastline indicates active wave attack today which is consistent with a rising level or falling land level. The sea has invaded the lower courses of these rivers and what we see today are the middle reaches. Reference to the photograph of Looe, Plate 3, shows clearly most of the features mentioned.

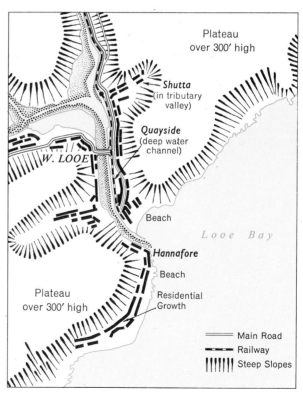

Approximate Scale 1:25,000

FIG. 33 Sketch-map showing position of West and East Looe.

Chapter Twelve: Glaciated Highlands: The Lake District Map 4

This map differs from the other maps in the book in that it is not part of a regular series covering the whole of the British Isles. For selected areas of great interest to the tourist, the Ordnance Survey have experimented with the portrayal of relief. The technique used on this Lake District map is that of oblique hill shading, with contours and layer colouring, discussed in Chapter 3.

Relief

A deeply dissected mountain area of England is seen on the map showing a great variety of landforms, presenting a more difficult problem in map interpretation.

The best way of describing this kind of map is to take in turn the constituent physical regions. These are given on Figure 34, and should be compared with the Block Diagram, Figure 35.

The Mountains

1a; 1b; 1c.

The highest peak is found in Region 1c (Pillar mountain 2,927 feet above sea-level), and the general summit level is well over 2,000 feet. The deep dissection of the upland blocks has produced several distinct peaks separated by saddles, cols and passes. In 1b the shallow saddles are well seen between Great Borne, Starling Dodd, and Red Pike. Black Sail Pass in 1c, Scarth Gap Pass in 1b, and Coledale Hause in 1a are good examples of cols. The term 'pass' is best kept for easy through-ways between mountain blocks.

The Valleys

2a; 2b.

The floors of the main valleys lie just below 400 feet giving an average relief over the map of approximately 2,000 feet. Note that the submarine contours show relief of the lake basins at 50 foot intervals. Crummock Water, for example, has an overall depth of 121 feet, which means that the depth of the lake basin is 200 feet above sea-level.

Drainage

The three main lakes and a small portion of a fourth constitute a principal feature of the map. Into the lake tumble numerous small, swift-flowing streams. The form of the lakes, their deep basins and their occurrence in deep valley troughs immediately suggest the work of ice.

Map Evidence of Glaciation

(a) The valley troughs are characteristically flat-floored, steep-sided and 'U' shaped.

(b) Arm-chair shaped hollows or corries—well seen at high levels with or without the small lake or tarn, e.g. Bleaberry Tarn (grid square 1615) and the north face of Pillar in Region 1c.

(c) Knife-edged ridges or arêtes separate many of the corries, e.g. Chapel Crags in 1b.

(d) Hanging valleys and waterfalls are identified by looking carefully at the contour pattern. The uppermost part of the valley will be a gentler gradient than the lower part and will appear to hang above the main valley trough. Sour Milk Ghyll (grid square 1615) is an excellent example.

(e) The main lakes in over-deepened rock basins.

These features are illustrated in Block Diagram and Map, Figures 21a and 21b. (Compare with Figure 35.)

The majority of the small streams draining into the lakes are normal young streams occupying 'V' shaped valleys cut since the Ice Age. The main rivers show interesting features, for example, the Liza is braided only four miles from its source, an indication of the flat glaciated valley and the misfit nature of the river.

The river draining Buttermere and Crummock Water flows slowly between the lakes and off the map to join eventually the Derwent. This river and many other streams are depositing rock material in these lakes, causing them in time to fill up. The pronounced flat to the west of Buttermere is probably the result of such deposition by Sail Beck and neighbouring streams. Similar areas are seen at the heads of Ennerdale Water, Buttermere and around the village of Loweswater.

Settlement

As might well be expected in such a hilly region, there is little settlement. There is none in the mountains and only limited settlement in the valleys, three very small villages and a few scattered dwellings.

Communications

No major road or railway can be seen. The minor roads are in Region IIa and are restricted to a very narrow strip of this valley floor. The road leaving the valley over Newlands Hause must negotiate three steep sections as indicated by gradient symbols. For the rest there are numerous footpaths linking by the easiest route neighbouring valleys.

Land Use

In a mountainous area of this kind Man's use of the land is necessarily limited by steep slopes, exposure to rough weather, great elevation, and difficult communications. The scattered dwellings marked on the map are probably farm houses though not one is named as such. We may only presume that valley flats are pastureland for cattle, and that the rough grazing of the lower slopes is used to raise flocks of sheep. An extensive coniferous plantation occupies almost the entire upper part of Ennerdale with the limit of tree growth about 1,250 feet. That the district is of great natural beauty can be seen at a glance; the National Trust preserves for the nation the three main lakes, one waterfall and several wooded and rocky places. The presence of Mountain Rescue Posts and Youth Hostels bears witness to the popularity of the region with walker and mountaineer.

Summary

The abundant surface water indicates impermeable rock outcrops but there is no map evidence at all to suggest the nature of the rock. Everywhere the signs of glaciation impress and provide some of the finest textbook examples of the work of ice in the British Isles. In this region there is a strong control over Man's activities by the dramatic form of the relief.

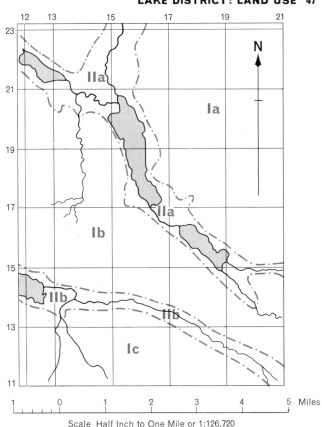

Fig. 34 Sketch-map to show physical regions of the Lake District map.

Scale Half Inch to One Mile or 1:126,720

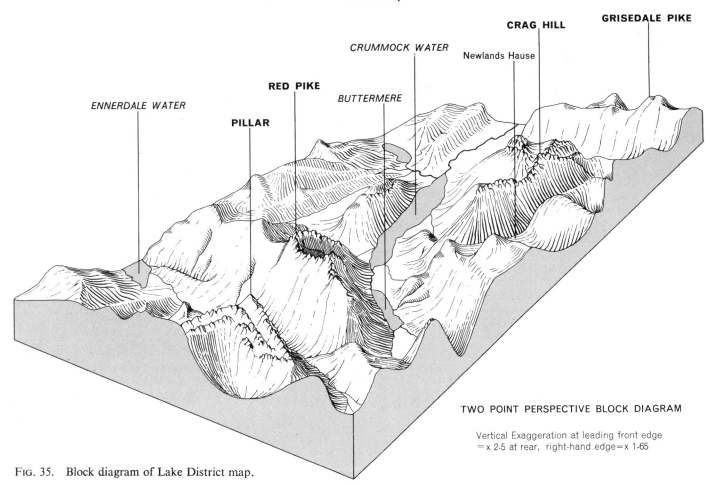

TWO POINT PERSPECTIVE BLOCK DIAGRAM

Vertical Exaggeration at leading front edge
= x 2·5 at rear, right-hand edge = x 1·65

Fig. 35. Block diagram of Lake District map.

Chapter Thirteen: A Limestone Upland: Ingleborough Map 5

This map shows part of the Pennines in north-west Yorkshire, drained by the Greta River which flows off the western edge of the map to join the River Lune.

Relief

A dissected upland block rises to over 2,000 feet above sea-level in Ingleborough Hill. The principal river valley is the Chapel Beck or Greta flowing in a general south-westerly direction. The river flows through a deep, flat-floored, steep-sided valley except in the lower reaches, shown on the map where the valley is more restricted. A close examination of the map suggests regional division as indicated in the sketch-map, Figure 36, 1a and 1b—the two related upland areas, and 2—the valley. The main physical features are illustrated on Block Diagram, Figure 37.

Region I

A platform can be seen generally above 1,000 feet in both hill masses, e.g. Scales Moor and White Scars. The edge of the platform is marked by the O.S. symbol for cliff-drawing indicating broken ground, bare rock, absence of soil and vegetation cover, e.g., Twistleton Scars and Raven Scars. The word 'scar' is a north-country term widely used to describe a steep rock outcrop. In Ib a steep-sided, flat-topped hill (Ingleborough Hill) rises abruptly from the platform too steep, in places, to be shown by contours and the cliff symbol is employed.

Region II

The river and its valley can be divided into two parts, above and below the crossing point of the river, at the ford, by the 675 foot contour (707748). The upper portion reveals a broad valley approximately half-mile wide in places with a gently flowing river. The valley is much narrower in the lower part, the river plunging through Twistleton Glen in a series of waterfalls.

Drainage

We can see at once the marked absence of streams in the uplands; the interrupted nature of the few that do exist suggests a surface rock of high degree of permeability. Closer study shows a marked spring-line on both flanks of the valley between 750-850 feet feeding the River Greta. For the rest of the upland Ia there is no other surface drainage at all. The comparable area of Ib shows a similar absence of drainage but numerous springs and short stream courses drain the high slopes of the Ingleborough massif. These streams originate in well marked springs just below the summit of Ingleborough and after a short swift course peter out. Mere Gill and Hard Gill terminate in pot-holes (swallowholes) at Spice Gill Hole and Rantry Hole. Other abandoned pot-holes are also marked, e.g. Braithwaite Wife Hole at 743762, which may take storm water.

The upper part of the Greta valley called Chapel Beck displays an unusual feature at God's Bridge (733764). The river at this point disappears for a short distance, providing a natural bridge used by a footpath.

FIG. 36 Sketch-map to show physical regions of the Ingleborough map.

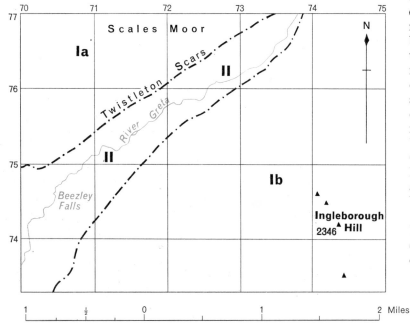

Scale 1 : 50,000 or about 1¼ Inches to One Mile

Settlement

Over the whole area of the map only eight major settlement points appear, all below 1,200 feet. These are isolated dwellings, almost certainly small farms, and occur at the break of slope between flood-plain and valley side.

Land Use

The floor of the main valley is divided into a mesh of small fields possibly devoted to pasture for cattle. The fields of the steeper slopes are noticeably larger and the rough nature of most of this country indicates the only possible farming activity is sheep raising. The summit areas are unfenced.

Some evidence of mining and quarrying is seen in the Lead Mines, e.g. grid square 7274 and the many quarries. (Lead often occurs as veins, in galena, lead sulphide, associated with limestone.) These mines are no longer operating. The main quarries are the 'Ingleton Granite Quarries' served by a mineral line and a road. It was noted in Chapter 5 that this rock is not granite but a rock with similar uses.

Communications

In a region of such low population density main railways and roads are not to be expected. Footpaths and trackways are the main links between settlements and the 'B' Class road avoids the valley floor, using the through way of the valley to join more distant places.

Summary

All the evidence points to a major rock outcrop of high permeability covering most of the upland as shown by the abundant evidence of underground drainage. The combination of pot-holes, springs, caves, scar edges, lead mines and the word 'limestone' is sufficient to conclude that this is massive limestone, the Carboniferous Limestone of England.

The River Greta and its numerous spring-heads indicate that the valley is floored by impermeable rock and the smaller streams at high levels show that there, too, impermeable strata can be found.

On the section Figure 14 the actual geology of the area is shown.

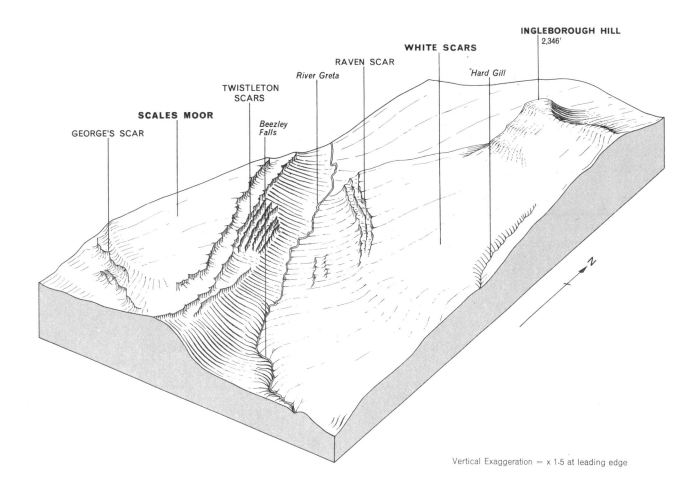

Vertical Exaggeration = x 1·5 at leading edge

FIG. 37   Block diagram of Ingleborough map.

Chapter Fourteen: Settlement and Communications: (A) Alloa Map 6

We can now turn from the analysis of relief and drainage and concentrate on settlement. This map extract of part of the East Central Lowlands includes in the north part of the Ochil Hills, one of a chain of igneous rock uplands forming the Northern Heights in the Midland Rift Valley of Scotland. It is clear that there has been a strong control by land and water features over the pattern of settlement and communications.

Settlement

There are no large towns to be seen on the map but many small nucleated settlements do appear. These include Alloa, a line of foothill towns, Alva, Tillicoultry and Dollar, and a few other scattered dwellings.

Alloa
The Site

This covers approximately one square mile between low hills and the River Forth; it is everywhere below the 100 foot contour line and is confined entirely to the north bank. The site takes advantage of a relatively deep water frontage (absence of mud shoals and sandbanks) at a point where the river begins to widen into the estuary.

The Situation

The river is very important to the town. Upstream to the north-west navigation would be difficult because of the numerous mud banks, sandbanks and islands. Bridge building appears to have been impossible until the railway era and it is noteworthy that Alloa Bridge selects a narrow channel between a peninsula of firm ground to the north, and a gravel bank to the south. A crossing-point from South Alloa to the main town would probably have hindered navigation and imposed considerable engineering difficulties.

Function

In spite of the absence of a road bridge the network of communications indicates the importance of the town, with its symbols showing both a main-line railway station and a bus and coach terminal. Port facilities include piers, open river docks, and a dock basin which are served by a dock railway. The evidence of industry is lacking, only the name 'Distillery' indicating an occupation.

The Foothill Towns

All are located on similar sites, and have the same situation with regard to relief.

The Site

It is remarkable how the small towns of Tillicoultry and Alva have sought out a narrow platform of raised ground encompassed by the 50 foot contour, lying well away from the river and flanked by steeply rising ground to the north. The factors that are probably responsible for the development of the site of Alva can be seen in Figure 28. The map shows that Tillicoultry has grown on a similar site and a study of Dollar reveals that although the general height is around 100 feet, the site characteristics are essentially the same as the other two towns.

The Situation

All three towns lie in the corridor of lowland in the valley of the River Devon on the northern margin of its floodplain between the low undulating hills in the middle of the map and the barrier of highlands to the north. Of minor importance perhaps in the situation of the three towns is the protection given by the highlands from northern gales, and the southerly aspect which favours sunshine and warmth.

Functions

These towns are too small to support much industry and the map evidence for it is scanty. A large factory at Menstrie, 858965, is served by a railway although the village is very small and the station closed to passengers. This suggests that Menstrie is a suburb of a larger town, or that workers are brought by road from some distance. Mill Glen, occupied by a fast-moving stream above Tillicoultry, may indicate an old industrial site and this town is the terminus of the main line section of the railway from Alloa, suggesting a place of some importance at the present time or at least in the recent past.

The other settlements on the map are scattered, and for the most part no more than small villages. Only Clackmannan and Tullibody deserve our attention. Clackmannan is a small nucleated settlement to the south of the Black Devon river, on the sides of a small knoll overlooking the Forth valley. A main road passes through the town but the village is served only by a single track railway and the station is closed. At Tullibody the form of the built-up area as shown by map symbols suggests a relatively modern development and this is confirmed somewhat by the absence of an old central nucleus and parish church. The railway by-passes the settlement well to the south.

Communications

We can appreciate best the pattern of communications by preparing a reduced sketch-map. Figure 38 shows clearly the strong control over the road and rail network exercised by the physical features. The highlands in the north prevent access by road and rail; only footpaths are shown in this northern area on the O.S. map. The uplands between the Devon and Forth valleys are nowhere high enough to prevent construction of roads and the railways can easily overcome the low gradients by means of short cuttings. As for

the influence of the main water channel, that of the Forth, reference has been made above to the problem of bridge construction and the navigational hazards of the river channel.

Summary

From his knowledge of the regional geography of Scotland the student should recognise in the name Clackmannan one of Scotland's five major coalfields, but on this map only one mine is marked, at Fishcross, 898958.

We have some reasons from the map for the settlement and communication layout of this part of the Scottish lowlands. The obvious physical control of the foothill towns and the limitation on the growth of Alloa imposed by the Forth River and its valley can be deduced from the map, but there is a marked lack of information relating to occupations.

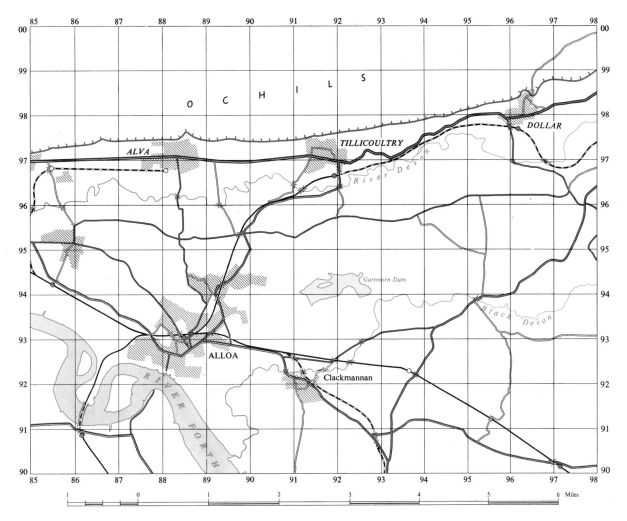

Scale: Three-Quarters of an Inch to One Mile

FIG. 38   Sketch-map of the communications on the map of Alloa.

Reproduced from the Ordnance Survey Map with the sanction of The Controller of H.M. Stationery Office.   Crown Copyright reserved.

Settlement (B) Aberystwyth Map 7

Aberystwyth is the largest town on the shores of Cardigan Bay in central Wales, occupying the lowland at the mouth of the River Rheidol. On this map the dominating position of Aberystwyth is at once evident and as a settlement study we can confine our interest to this town.

Site

This seaside town occupies a relatively restricted site between upland country inland and the river itself. The central part of the town occupies a shallow depression extending down to the beach. The western part of the town is limited by the rocky foreshore and cliffs, and the small knoll on which stands the remains of an old castle. To the east and north the town sprawls up the lower slopes of the hills and the formation of a small tributary valley, whilst to the south the mud-flats have prevented much expansion on this side of the river. Trefechan has developed on a small flat at the foot of Pendinas Hill, and the deposition of a shingle spit has obstructed access to the sea, but it can be seen that the river is still tidal to a point one mile inland. We might expect in such a sheltered position that a small harbour would grow up. The only map evidence is a pier to support this conclusion.

Situation

On this lowland site at the terminus of the broad corridor of the Rheidol valley the settlement of Aberystwyth has probably grown around the lowest bridging point where the combined waters of two rivers may have encouraged fishing and other port activities. The presence of a castle, now in ruins, supports this theory, standing as it does overlooking the river mouth and commanding all approaches to the valley.

Aberystwyth then has become a natural focus of roads which follow upland routes. On the other hand, the two railways of much later date have been constructed in the valleys. The two obvious reasons for the present-day importance of the town are its functions as a seaside resort and centre of a Welsh university.

In the Welsh language ABER-YSTWYTH means mouth of the river YSTWYTH, yet the principal bridge leading into the town is over the River RHEIDOL.

Figure 39 shows that the old site of Aberystwyth was above 25 feet (around the castle) and that the newer suburbs have spread across lower ground to the hill slopes beyond. Trefechan is below 25 feet and only

just above high water suggesting a later origin possibly following the construction of a bridge from Aberystwyth.

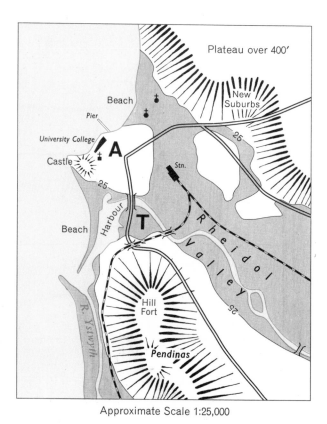

Approximate Scale 1:25,000

A Aberystwyth ||||||| Steep Slopes
T Trefechan   ═══ Main Road
   ▬■▬ Railway

FIG. 39 Sketch-map showing the site and situation of Aberystwyth.

Chapter Fifteen: An Industrial Location: Skinningrove Map 8

In the British Isles most industrial areas are densely populated and the industries highly concentrated. This map shows one of the few exceptions—a village with a large scale industry. All the industrial plant is readily seen on this map drawn on a scale of six inches to one mile. The location is in north-east Yorkshire on the flanks of the North York Moors, facing across the sea.

It is possible to distinguish on this scale different types of building: (1) industrial plant, (2) dwelling houses along named streets; (3) public buildings, e.g. churches and schools.

1. Industrial Plant

We can see that the main factory buildings occupy a site roughly 500 yards by 200 yards, but if we include spoil heaps, railway sidings and other services, the area covers nearly one-quarter of the map. The main buildings extend over a raised site on the west flank of a steep-sided valley (with care the river can be traced by following upstream from the mouth, which is clearly seen in Cattersty Sands), terminating seawards in cliffs rising to 200 feet. The two major works and the smaller factories are aligned parallel to the numerous railway tracks. Clearly these tracks serve different purposes and a close study reveals their function:

(a) A track from the jetty to the works for the movement of raw materials and finished goods.
(b) tracks joining the main line at Carlin How Junction serving the same purpose.
(c) tracks leading from the works to the extensive tip heaps.
(d) tracks running through the plant.

Other tracks serve mines, both drift and shaft, in the valley bottom. The absence of good roads in the vicinity of the works and the presence of a dense railway network tells us that heavy bulk goods are being transported.

Other named evidence of industry in this area includes references to Works, Mines, Shafts, Drifts.

From the foregoing evidence we can eliminate many industrial activities, e.g. textiles and car manufacturing. Extensive spoil heaps and railway tracks mean a heavy refining industry, such as chemicals or iron and steel. The lay-out of the plant points to iron and steel since chemicals are generally manufactured in scattered buildings and require special storage facilities. The mines shown could serve the works with any of its three raw materials: ore, limestone and coal. There is no evidence which of these materials is actually extracted.

2. Dwelling Houses

These are very typical of 19th Century Industrial Dwellings built in long terraced rows close to the place of employment.

3. Public Buildings

Three schools and three churches represent all the evidence of important public buildings.

The character of the industrial site and the nature of the industry is brought out clearly by the photograph, Plate 8. This is taken from behind Skinningrove Farm at 719196. Pay particular attention to the following:

(1) The plateau top site extending to the cliff edge,
(2) the blast furnace and gas retorts,
(3) an extensive industrial lay-out, suggesting an integrated iron and steel works,
(4) the isolation of the works in an otherwise rural area (The houses of the village are hidden from view in the photograph),
(5) the typical north country farm house built of local stone.

Hints for the Examination

1. Go to the Examination Room fully equipped with drawing instruments—pen, pencils (H.B. and H.), one-foot rule, compasses, dividers, protractors, coloured crayons, eraser.
2. Where the examination paper provides 15 minutes for scrutiny of the map use this time to check questions against the map evidence and locate grid references. Do not waste time with the other questions on the paper.
3. Note the scale of the map extract.
4. Distance measurement—on the 1 : 25,000 map calculate distances using the R.F.: on the one inch map use the scale lines.
5. Direction. Draw in the direction required on the map and remember—' of ', ' from ' and ' between ' are the important words.
6. Section drawing. Is a cross-section or sketch section required? If cross-section is required use graph paper when provided and transfer contour heights direct to block. If no vertical scale is given use one-tenth of an inch to 50 feet.
7. Intervisibility. This must be determined by a cross-section.
8. Gradients. $\dfrac{\text{V.I. (in feet)}}{\text{H.D. (in feet)}}$ and state as 1 in ——.
9. Reductions to half scale:
   (a) Reduce map-framework to half-size,
   (b) Insert grid lines,
   (c) Trace in detail with reference to grid lines,
   (d) Draw new scale or add new R.F.
   (Multiply original denominator by two.)
10. Physical Regions. To divide an area choose a significant contour to separate upland and lowland. Either give names, or numbers and a key, to describe the actual land-forms shown.
    To describe sub-regions indicate the height, slope, drainage, nature of surface, aspect, and suggest rock type.
11. Settlement. Distinguish between (i) site and (ii) situation or position; the simplest answer is to draw and label a sketch-map. Look for settlement types, e.g. spring-line villages, but remember several factors may account for their origin.
12. Communications. Give a simple sketch-map to show the road and rail pattern; do not forget other forms, e.g. rivers and canals, seaports, airports.

Scale 1 : 63,360 : 1 Inch to 1 Mile. Seventh Series

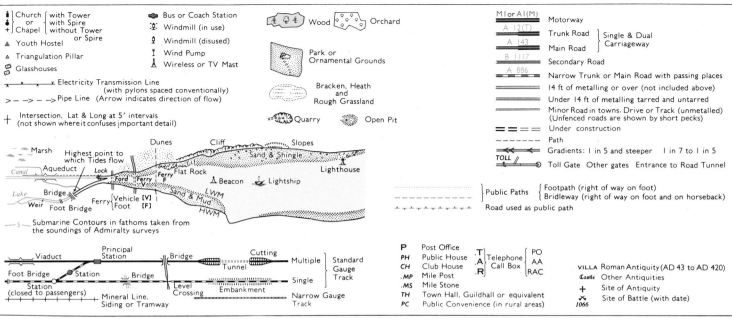

Church or Chapel { with Tower / with Spire / without Tower or Spire }
▲ Youth Hostel
△ Triangulation Pillar
⌂ Glasshouses

Electricity Transmission Line (with pylons spaced conventionally)
> — > — —> Pipe Line (Arrow indicates direction of flow)
+ Intersection, Lat & Long at 5' intervals (not shown where it confuses important detail)

Bus or Coach Station
Windmill (in use)
Windmill (disused)
Wind Pump
Wireless or TV Mast

Wood   Orchard
Park or Ornamental Grounds
Bracken, Heath and Rough Grassland
Quarry   Open Pit

Marsh
Highest point to which Tides flow
Canal Aqueduct Lock
Lake Bridge Ford Ferry Ferry Flat Rock
Weir Foot Bridge Ferry { Vehicle [V] / Foot [F] }
Dunes Cliff Slopes
Sand & Shingle
Lighthouse
Beacon Lightship
Sand & Mud LWM HWM
— 5 — Submarine Contours in fathoms taken from the soundings of Admiralty surveys

Viaduct Principal Station Bridge Cutting
Foot Bridge Station Bridge Tunnel Multiple } Standard Gauge Track
Station (closed to passengers) Level Crossing Single
Mineral Line, Siding or Tramway Embankment Narrow Gauge Track

M1 or A1(M) Motorway
A 12(T) Trunk Road } Single & Dual Carriageway
A 143 Main Road
B 1117 Secondary Road
A 886 Narrow Trunk or Main Road with passing places
14 ft of metalling or over (not included above)
Under 14 ft of metalling tarred and untarred
Minor Road in towns. Drive or Track (unmetalled) (Unfenced roads are shown by short pecks)
Under construction
Path
Gradients: 1 in 5 and steeper 1 in 7 to 1 in 5
TOLL Toll Gate Other gates Entrance to Road Tunnel

——————— } Public Paths { Footpath (right of way on foot) / Bridleway (right of way on foot and on horseback)
+ + + + + + + Road used as public path

P Post Office
PH Public House
CH Club House
.MP Mile Post
.MS Mile Stone
TH Town Hall, Guildhall or equivalent
PC Public Convenience (in rural areas)

T / A / R } Telephone Call Box { PO / AA / RAC

VILLA Roman Antiquity (AD 43 to AD 420)
Castle Other Antiquities
+ Site of Antiquity
⚔ Site of Battle (with date)
1066

Scale 1 : 25,000 : 2½ Inches to 1 Mile. Second Series

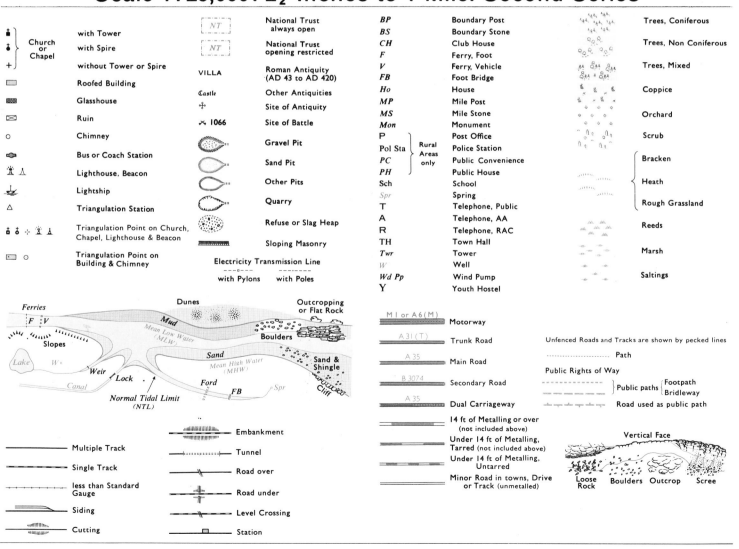

Church or Chapel { with Tower / with Spire / without Tower or Spire }
Roofed Building
Glasshouse
Ruin
Chimney
Bus or Coach Station
Lighthouse, Beacon
Lightship
Triangulation Station
Triangulation Point on Church, Chapel, Lighthouse & Beacon
Triangulation Point on Building & Chimney

NT National Trust always open
NT National Trust opening restricted
VILLA Roman Antiquity (AD 43 to AD 420)
Castle Other Antiquities
+ Site of Antiquity
⚔ 1066 Site of Battle
Gravel Pit
Sand Pit
Other Pits
Quarry
Refuse or Slag Heap
Sloping Masonry
Electricity Transmission Line with Pylons / with Poles

BP Boundary Post
BS Boundary Stone
CH Club House
F Ferry, Foot
V Ferry, Vehicle
FB Foot Bridge
Ho House
MP Mile Post
MS Mile Stone
Mon Monument
P Post Office } Rural Areas only
Pol Sta Police Station
PC Public Convenience
PH Public House
Sch School
Spr Spring
T Telephone, Public
A Telephone, AA
R Telephone, RAC
TH Town Hall
Twr Tower
W Well
Wd Pp Wind Pump
Y Youth Hostel

Trees, Coniferous
Trees, Non Coniferous
Trees, Mixed
Coppice
Orchard
Scrub
Bracken
Heath
Rough Grassland
Reeds
Marsh
Saltings

M1 or A6(M) Motorway
A31(T) Trunk Road
A 35 Main Road
B 3074 Secondary Road
A 35 Dual Carriageway
14 ft of Metalling or over (not included above)
Under 14 ft of Metalling, Tarred (not included above)
Under 14 ft of Metalling, Untarred
Minor Road in towns, Drive or Track (unmetalled)

Unfenced Roads and Tracks are shown by pecked lines
.... Path
Public Rights of Way
————— } Public paths { Footpath / Bridleway
+ + + + Road used as public path

Ferries
F V
Slopes Dunes Mud Outcropping or Flat Rock
Mean Low Water (MLW) Boulders
Lake W
Weir Lock Sand Mean High Water (MHW) Sand & Shingle
Canal Ford Cliff
Normal Tidal Limit (NTL) FB Spr

Embankment
Tunnel
Road over
Road under
Level Crossing
Station

Multiple Track
Single Track
less than Standard Gauge
Siding
Cutting

Vertical Face
Loose Rock Boulders Outcrop Scree

Reproduced from the Ordnance Survey Maps with the sanction of the Controller of H.M. Stationery Office. Crown Copyright reserved.

Question Paper 1 — Map 1

1. (a) State the distance in miles and furlongs by road, and the direction, between Stanway church (061323) and Broadway church (095373).

   (b) Identify the O.S. symbols given at the following Grid References: 048325; 075384; 118383; 096337; 114336; 016324; and between 063353 and 056339.

   (c) Calculate the average gradient of the track leading from the Camp at 081335 to Stanton Village at 067341.

2. Describe the course of the A44 road from the eastern edge of the map to Broadway continuing south by the A46.

3. Describe in detail the course of the main north-south railway.

4. Describe the distribution of orchards on the map and suggest reasons for their situation.

Question Paper 2 — Map 1

1. (a) Reduce the map-extract to half scale, as outlined in Chapter 2, and insert the following: (i) 250 foot contour line; (ii) River Isbourne. Add short linear scale, the Representative Fraction and an orientation sign.

   The map falls into three physical regions— the dissected upland, the lowland, and an isolated knoll.

   (b) Print boldly on the map, in appropriate places, the following terms: back or dip slope; scarp face; outlier; vale; one example of a dry valley; and by a dotted line insert and name the watershed.

2. Draw a cross-section from 000350 to 130322, and by symbols indicate the nature of the rocks; mark by arrows and name where the section crosses a major river; a footpath; a major road; a tributary; a main railway line and an area of mixed woodland.

3. (a) Describe the site and situation of Broadway.

   (b) Suggest reasons for its growth as the largest settlement on the map.

Supplementary Questions — Map 1

1. Using the Representative Fraction only, work out, to the nearest square mile the total area covered by the map.

2. Give Normal Kilometre Grid References for one example of each of the following: trigonometrical Station; mile post; viaduct; earthwork; inn; Manor House.

3. State the direction: (a) by points of the compass; (b) by angular bearing; of the Golf Club House (119384) from spot height 443 (025315), and between the two National Trust properties shown on the map.

4. Cover the map with tracing paper and mark off the River Isbourne, all the minor streams and other water features, e.g. ponds, lakes, moats. Is there any evidence suggesting how the upland farms obtain their water supplies?

5. Describe the physical features crossed on a walk from Laverton, via Shenberrow Hill to Stanway, using footpaths and trackways only.

6. Explain in detail why a tunnel was constructed on the railway line in Grid Square 0130.

7. Determine by construction of a cross-section whether the Halt on the railway line at Gretton (005305) can be seen from the top of Oat Hill (096335).

8. Draw a sketch-map dividing the uplands and lowlands by the 250 foot contour line. Mark in the approximate crest of the escarpment by a bold line and then enter on the map, by suitable symbols, all the evidence for Roman and prehistoric settlement.

9. Draw separate sketch-maps to show the sites of Broadway and Stanton and suggest reasons for the growth of Stanton.

10. Consult an Atlas and find out the destinations of the major roads leaving the edges of the map.

11. On tracing paper draw the outline of the parish of Stanton. Mark and name the main physical regions, viz. the vale, the scarp face and the crest of the escarpment. Write notes on the nature of the land surface and the way it is used in each region.

12. Imagine this area flooded to a depth of 250 feet above sea-level. Describe the changes brought about in the landscape by this rise.

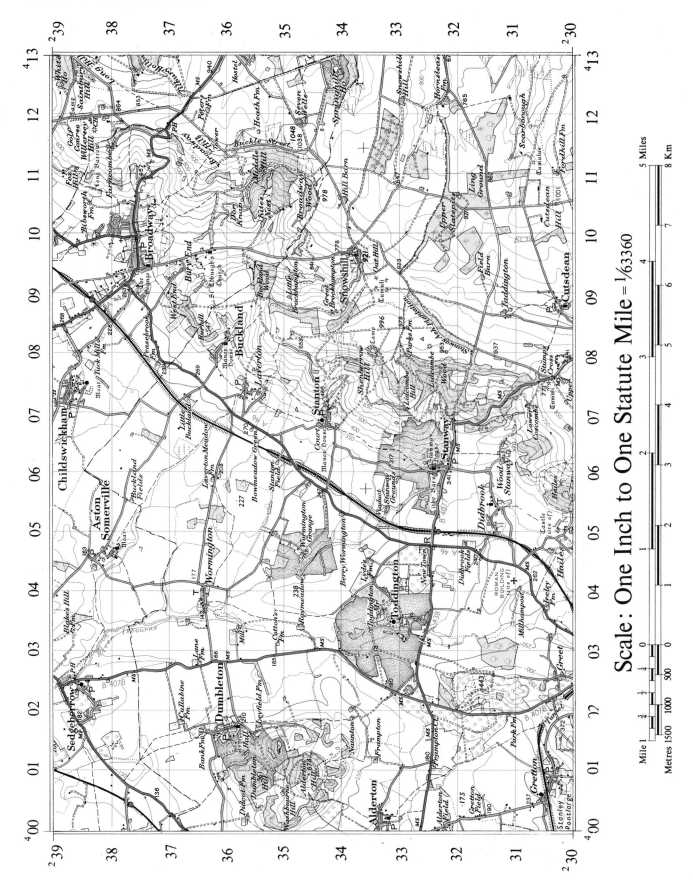

Scale: One Inch to One Statute Mile = 1/63360

Reproduced from the Ordnance Survey Map with the sanction of The Controller of H.M. Stationery Office.   Crown Copyright reserved.

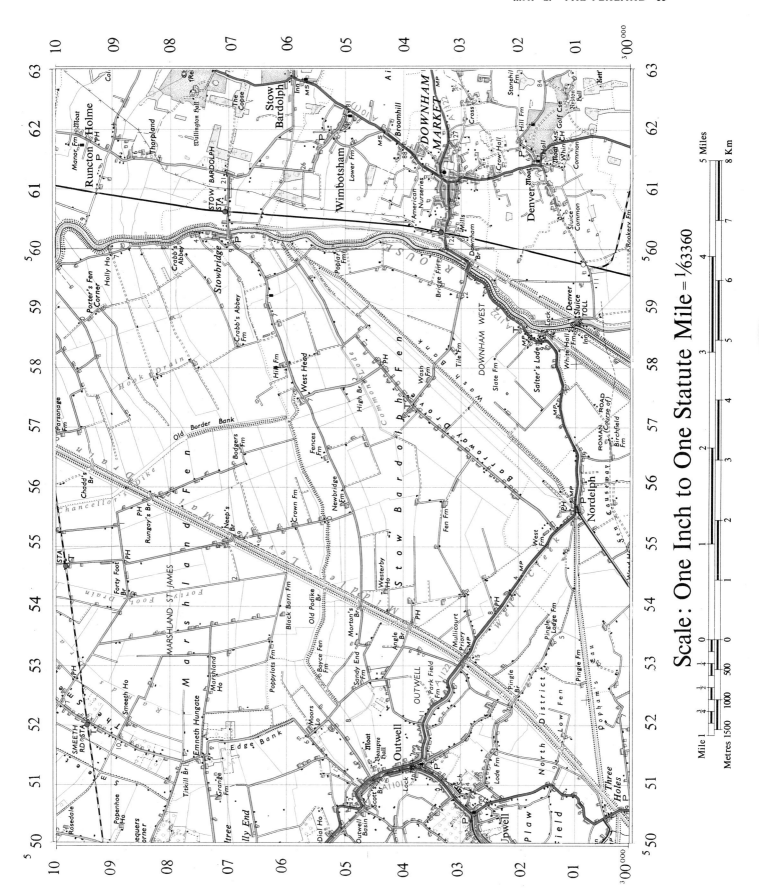

Scale: One Inch to One Statute Mile = 1/63360

Reproduced from the Ordnance Survey Map with the sanction of The Controller of H.M. Stationery Office.   Crown Copyright reserved.

Question Paper 1 — Map 2

1. Write an account of the drainage channels seen on the map under the headings: (a) natural water-courses; (b) field drains; (c) main drains.
2. Explain briefly the functions of the Sluice and Locks at 588010.
3. Describe the shape and site of the villages of Outwell and Upwell.
4. Suggest reasons for the growth of the settlement at Downham Market.

Question Paper 2 — Map 2

1. On a sketch-map of the area given on the map-extract indicate clearly the following: 50 foot contour line; the River Ouse; the Middle Level Main Drain; three sites at sea-level; a section of narrow-gauge railway; a disused wind-mill probably used formerly for pumping.
2. On an enlarged sketch-map show all the drainage features and flood control on the River Ouse between Denver Sluice and Downham Bridge.
3. Attempt to account for the growth of the villages of Denver, Wimbotsham, and Stow Bardolph.
4. Outline the map evidence that suggests that this is an important farming area.

Supplementary Questions — Map 2

1. List three pieces of map evidence that clearly reveal that most of the land shown on the map is about sea-level.
2. Indicate any difficulties likely to arise in the farming of Stow Bardolph Fen.
3. Describe the course of the A1122 from Scott's Bridge in Outwell to Salter's Lode.
4. Suggest a reason for the marked bends in the road to the north-west of Outwell.
5. Why would you consider that the settlement at Runcton Holme 6109 is older than that at Barroway Drove 5602-5804?
   Using vertical air photograph, Plate II and the map:
6. State by means of six-figure grid references the locations of points A, B and C marked on the photograph.
7. Examine closely the course taken by the river Ouse and the drainage channels nearby. State the evidence that indicates that the map of this area is now out-of-date.
8. Give reasons why most of the fields around the villages of Upwell and Outwell are smaller than those in the rest of the fen.
9. The additional information on the photograph confirms that this area is one of intensive arable farming. List the evidence in support of this statement.
10. By careful measurement on both map and photograph, calculate the scale of the photograph and state by the Representative Fraction.

Question Paper 1 — Map 3

1. Reduce the map extract to half-scale, inserting the following:
   (a) the coastline as shown by H.W.M.O.T.,
   (b) the two main rivers,
   (c) a sandy beach,
   (d) the 300 foot contour line,
   (e) marsh area.
2. Construct a cross-section from trigonometrical station at 242548 to the trigonometrical station at 262543.
3. Using the cross-section obtained in Question 2, give reasons to account for the shape of the valley floor and the valley sides.
4. Describe the nature of the coastal forms.

Question Paper 2 — Map 3

1. State in miles and yards the distance ' as the crow flies ' of the trigonometrical station 242548 from the trigonometrical station on St. George's or Looe Island 257514.
2. Describe in detail what you would see from a yacht sailing from the harbour mouth up the East Looe River.
3. Comment on the distribution and type of woodland shown on the map.
4. Draw a sketch-map to show the position and importance of West and East Looe.

Supplementary Questions — Map 3

1. On a tracing of the map outline indicate the following by printing boldly in suitable places the words:
   Young Valley; Spur; Meanders; Convex Slope; Stack; Wave-cut Platform.
2. Refer to the map and locate on the photograph (Plate 3) the features to be seen at the following Grid References: 257530; 258528; 252539; 254539; 258534–258536.
3. Suggest, giving at least two reasons, the season of the year, and one reason for the time of day when the photograph was taken.
4. What photographic evidence is there of:
   (a) use of land for farming,
   (b) tourist industry,
   (c) port activities.
5. Describe the vegetation as seen on the photograph and compare with the symbols drawn on the map.
6. Describe the course of the main road across the map.
7. Draw diagrams to illustrate the formation of Looe Island.
8. What mileages are likely to appear on the guide post in St. Martin? State the destinations of the three road indicators.

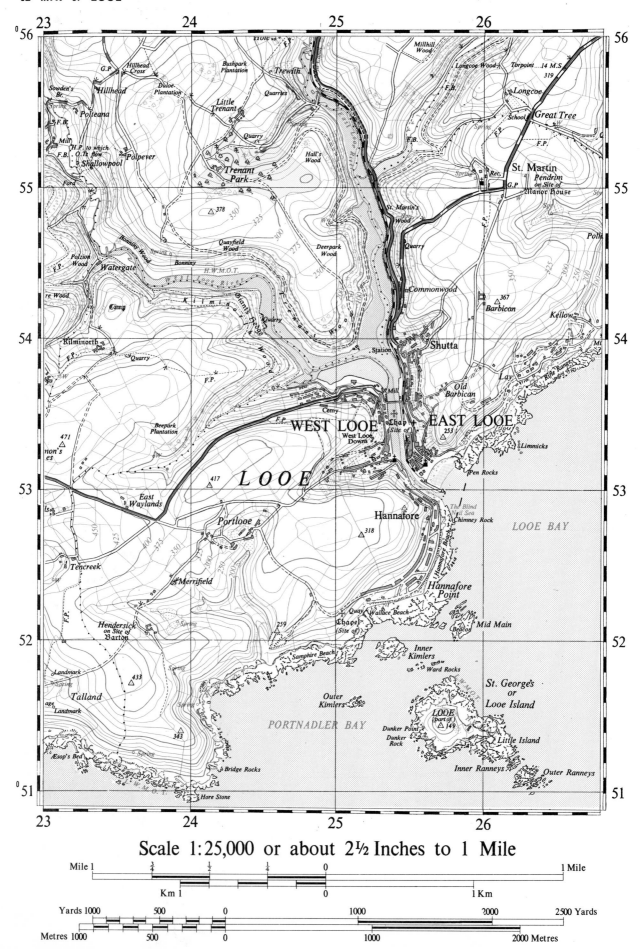

Scale 1:25,000 or about 2½ Inches to 1 Mile

Mile 1   ¾   ½   ¼   0   1 Mile

Km 1   0   1 Km

Yards 1000   500   0   1000   2000   2500 Yards

Metres 1000   500   0   1000   2000 Metres

Reproduced from the Ordnance Survey Map with the sanction of The Controller of H.M. Stationery Office.   Crown Copyright reserved.

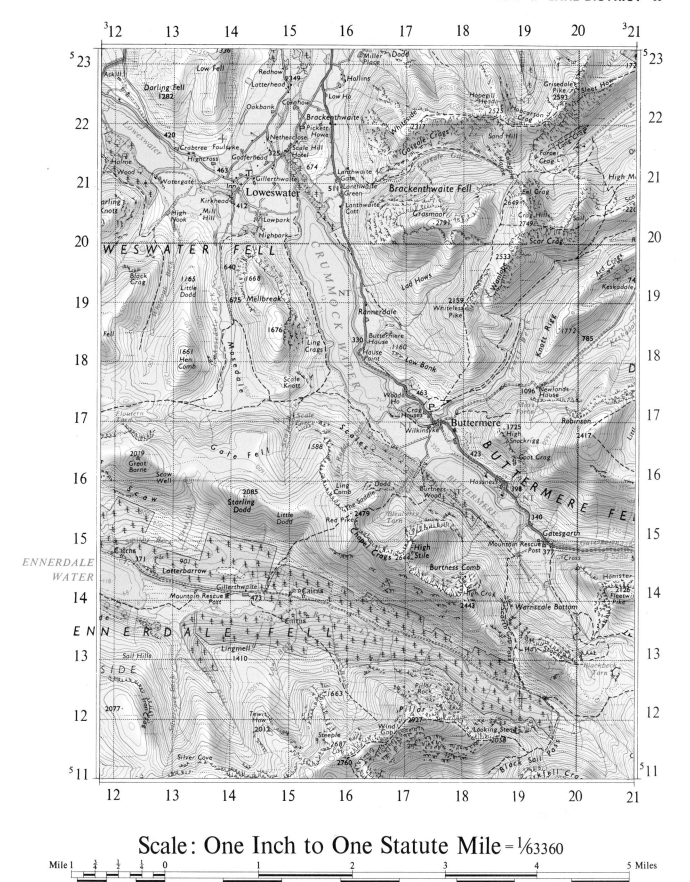

Scale: One Inch to One Statute Mile = 1/63360

Mile 1   3/4   1/2   1/4   0   1   2   3   4   5 Miles

Metres 1500 1000 500 0   1   2   3   4   5   6   7   8 Km

Reproduced from the Ordnance Survey Map with the sanction of The Controller of H.M. Stationery Office.   Crown Copyright reserved.

Question Paper 1 — Map 4

1. Draw a sketch-section from the summit of Robinson (202168) to the summit of High Stile (170147) and indicate clearly the lake, an arête, a minor road and a wood.
2. Calculate the average gradient of Sour Milk Ghyll from its exit from Bleaberry Tarn to its point of entry into the lake.
3. Confining your attention to the north-eastern corner of the map draw a sketch-map indicating the glaciated features by symbol and correct physical name.
4. What are the map signs that this is a popular tourist area?

Question Paper 2 — Map 4

1. Calculate the distance in miles and furlongs from the Mountain Rescue Post at Gatesgarth (195149) to the Youth Hostel at Gillerthwaite (139141) following the footpath over Scarth Gap and the trackway down the Liza.
2. Determine whether you could see the church in Buttermere Village from the summit of Pillar mountain (171121).
3. Describe the site of Buttermere Village.
4. Describe in detail the physical features to be seen on the route measured in Question 1.

Supplementary Questions — Map 4

1. Explain why Man's activities are exclusively confined to the valleys.
2. Write an account of land use in Ennerdale.
3. Comment on the boundaries of the National Trust Property and suggest reasons for their distribution.
4. What is the elevation above sea-level of the floor of Lake Buttermere?
5. Compare with the aid of simple sketch-sections the form of the valleys of Sail Beck and Crummock Water-Buttermere.
6. Calculate to the nearest square mile the area of the north-eastern upland block bounded by the 500 foot contour.
7. Make lists of the occurrence of the place-names: Dodd; Beck; Pike; Hause and Thwaite and suggest from the map evidence their meanings.
8. List all the ways in which relief is shown on this map.
9. Examine the photograph of the lakes and:
   (a) State the direction from which the photograph was taken.
   (b) Locate by Grid References two large houses to the right-hand side of the lake in the foreground.
10. Using the map and photograph together attempt an explanation of the flat land lying between the two lakes Buttermere and Crummock Water. (The small delta in the left foreground of the photograph should provide a clue to the processes involved.)

Question Paper 1 — Map 5

1. Calculate to the nearest 100 yards the distance between Twistleton Hall (702751) via the ford (715753) and Lancaster.
2. State the area of the map to the nearest square mile.
3. (a) Draw sections across the Greta Valley from The Spring (701752) to Flagstaff (714738); and Standing Stone (707765) to Trigonometrical Station (727747).
   Mark and name the river and the road.
      Use a vertical scale of 1/10 inch to represent 50 feet and the horizontal scale of the map.
      Mark and name one important physical feature and one human feature on each section.
   (b) How do the sections bring out the characteristic features of the valley?
4. Describe the features you would see on a journey along the route given in Question 1 to the edge of the map.

Question Paper 2 — Map 5

1. Calculate the distance ' as the crow flies,' and the direction of Dale Barn (712753) from the trigonometrical station on Ingleborough Hill (743744).
2. Draw to half-scale a sketch-map of the area shown and on it mark accurately the following: River Greta, a waterfall, 900 foot contour line, the summit of Ingleborough Hill, the course of Mere Gill, two potholes. Shade and name a platform and a spur.
   Indicate by symbols the outcrop of major rock scars.
3. Starting from Skirwith (707738) and following field boundaries to the footpath in Crina Bottom and thence to the summit of Ingleborough, describe the physical and man-made features you would see in the immediate vicinity of the route.
4. What features would you expect to see underground at Braithwaite Wife Hole?

Supplementary Questions — Map 5

Using the photograph, Plate V and the map:
1. State the direction in which the camera was pointing and locate by grid references the quarry shown in the photograph.
2. Examine the limestone scars on the photograph and from the contours of the map find their average height.
3. Describe the ways in which the mineral is extracted and removed from the quarry.
4. Examine the occurrence of springs on both sides of the valley at high and low levels and by referring to the geological section, Figure 37, suggest reasons for their location.

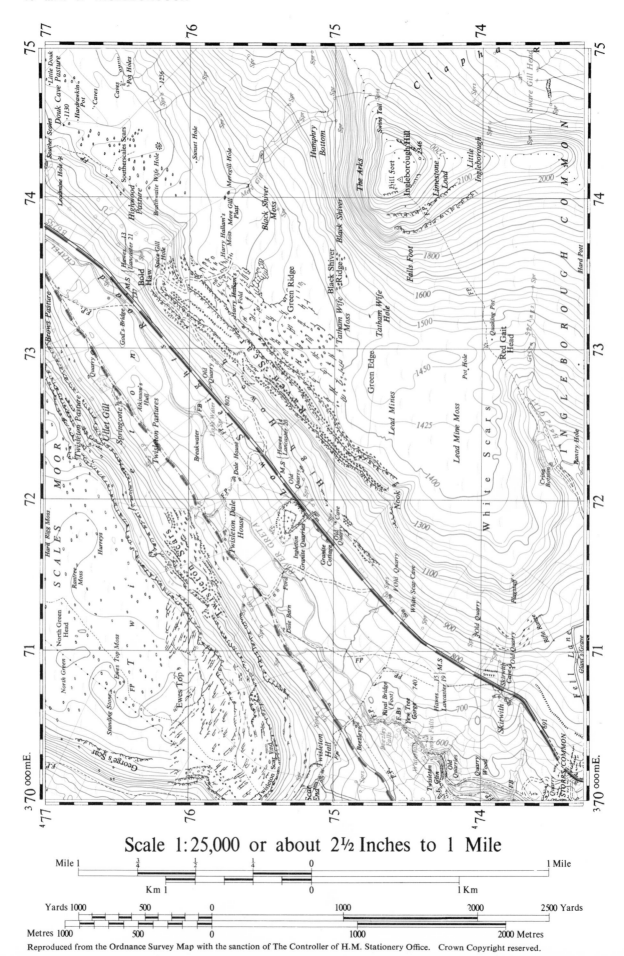

Scale 1:25,000 or about 2½ Inches to 1 Mile

Mile 1   ¾   ½   ¼   0   1 Mile

Km 1   0   1 Km

Yards 1000   500   0   1000   2000   2500 Yards

Metres 1000   500   0   1000   2000 Metres

Reproduced from the Ordnance Survey Map with the sanction of The Controller of H.M. Stationery Office.   Crown Copyright reserved.

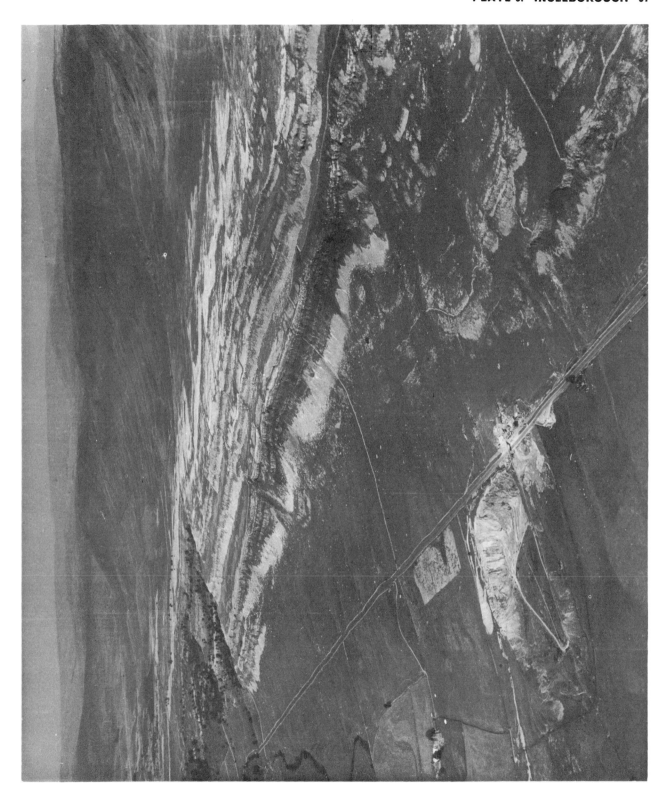

Question Paper 1 — Map 6

1. (a) Draw a sketch-map of the area shown and divide into physical regions. Add appropriate physical names to each region.
   (b) Compare the physical features of the valleys of the rivers Devon and Forth.
2. Find good examples of each of the following, quoting grid references in each case: Ox-bow Lake; Sand Bank; Rock Outcrop; Viaduct; Club House; Spoil Heap.
3. Describe the course taken by the railway from 867900 through Alloa to the station at Dollar.
4. Produce a sketch-map to illustrate concisely the site of Alloa.

Question Paper 2 — Map 6

1. State: (a) the direction of Calsnair Hill (861993), from New Sauchie church (897945);
   (b) the shortest distance by: (i) road, (ii) rail from the main line station in Alloa to the station at Dollar.
2. Relate the distribution of woodland shown on the map to both elevation and relief.
3. Calculate the gradient of the small stream in grid square 8797, terminating at the secondary road near the Golf Course.
4. Describe the site and the situation of Dollar, and account for its growth.

Supplementary Questions — Map 6

1. What is the depth in feet of Gartmorn Dam, 9194 and 9294?
2. Find examples of:
   (i) Parish boundaries,
   (ii) County and parish boundaries,
   (iii) Electricity transmission lines,
   (iv) Scottish National Trust properties,
   (v) Ancient monuments,
   Locate each example by grid reference,
3. What stage of river development is shown by the part of the River Devon that appears on the map? Give reasons for your answer.
4. Examine closely the distribution of small mineral working lines and railway lines in relation to the most likely industrial development in the region.
5. Locate the area shown on the photograph, Plate VI, and name the settlements shown.
6. Give four-figure grid references for the following:
   (i) the factory block in the foreground,
   (ii) the graveyard in the foreground,
   (iii) the triangular-shaped housing estate to the extreme right in the middle distance,
   (iv) a railway engine in full steam,
   (v) the isolated farm in the left middle distance.
7. State the differences between the valley of the River Devon and the Silver Glen.
8. Explain how the photograph supplements map information about land-use in this area.

Question Paper 1 — Map 7

1. Reduce the map to half-scale and on it insert the 100 foot contour line.
   This divides the map into three upland regions and two river valleys. Number the uplands from north to south: 1A, 1B, 1C, and the valleys 2A, 2B.
2. Compare and contrast the physical features of the two valleys.
3. Write briefly on the distribution and type of settlement in Region 1B, excluding the suburbs of Aberystwyth.
4. Explain the advantages possessed by Aberystwyth as a seaside resort.

Question Paper 2 — Map 7

1. Construct a cross-section, using graph paper, from Wellington Monument 584802 to the Guide Post 600822 and on it mark and name: the River Rheidol; a main road; narrow-gauge railway.
2. Describe in detail a walk along the entire coast shown on the map.
3. Indicate the reasons for the absence of settlement at the mouth of the Dyffryn Clarach.
4. Explain why recent expansion of building in Aberystwyth does not appear to move up the valley of the Rheidol.

Supplementary Questions — Map 7

1. What evidence is there on the map of a Welsh university town?
2. Describe the distribution of extractive industries seen on the map.
3. Draw a sketch-map indicating the site of Llanbadarn-Fawr, (600809) and suggest reasons for its growth.
4. Find examples of each of the following, locating by means of grid references:
   (i) a slope with a gradient greater than 1 in 3,
   (ii) a cliff over 300 feet high,
   (iii) section of sandy beach,
   (iv) evidence of prehistoric occupation.
5. Identify the following features indicated by grid references: 598814; 598821; 583825 to 584828; 602839; 582826.
6. Using map and photograph, Plate 7, draw a sketch-map to show the site of Trefechan and describe the plan of the buildings.
7. What can be seen on the photograph at the following grid references taken from the map: 584827; 584812; 583812; 581814; 586818.
8. Suggest, with reasons, the state of the tide when the photograph was taken.

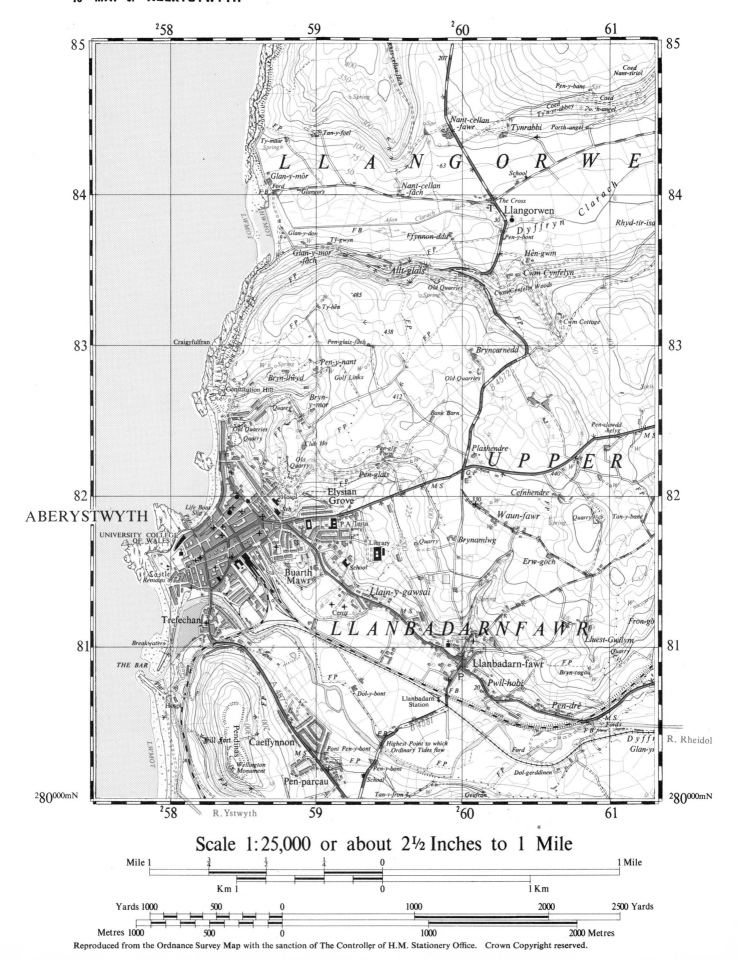

Scale 1:25,000 or about 2½ Inches to 1 Mile

Reproduced from the Ordnance Survey Map with the sanction of The Controller of H.M. Stationery Office.   Crown Copyright reserved.

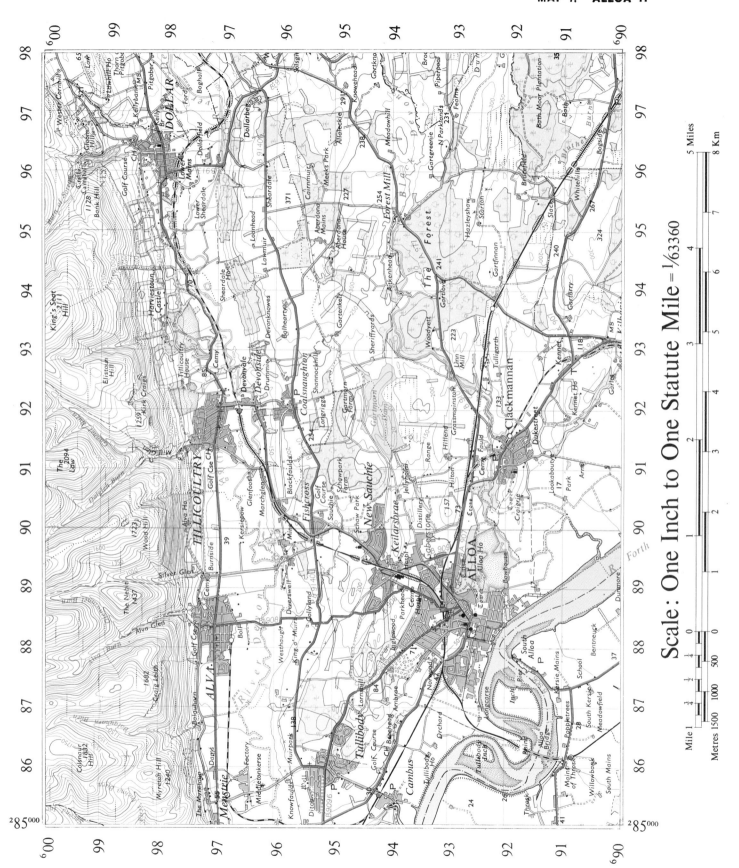

Scale: One Inch to One Statute Mile = ¹/₆₃₃₆₀

Reproduced from the Ordnance Survey Map with the sanction of The Controller of H.M. Stationery Office.   Crown Copyright reserved.

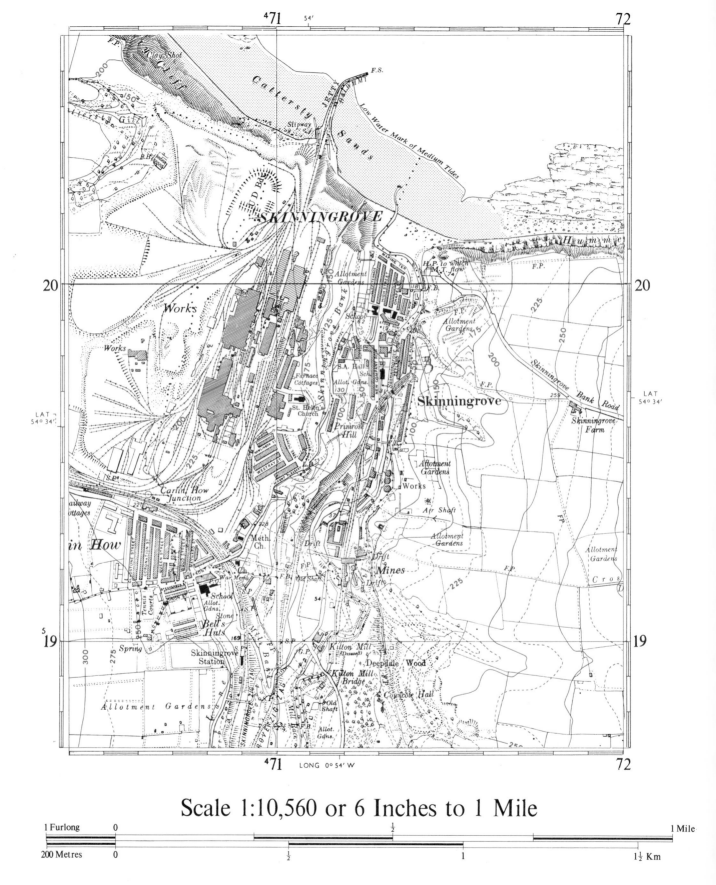

Scale 1:10,560 or 6 Inches to 1 Mile

1 Furlong   0   ½   1 Mile

200 Metres   0   ½   1   1½ Km

Reproduced from the Ordnance Survey Map with the sanction of The Controller of H.M. Stationery Office.   Crown Copyright reserved.

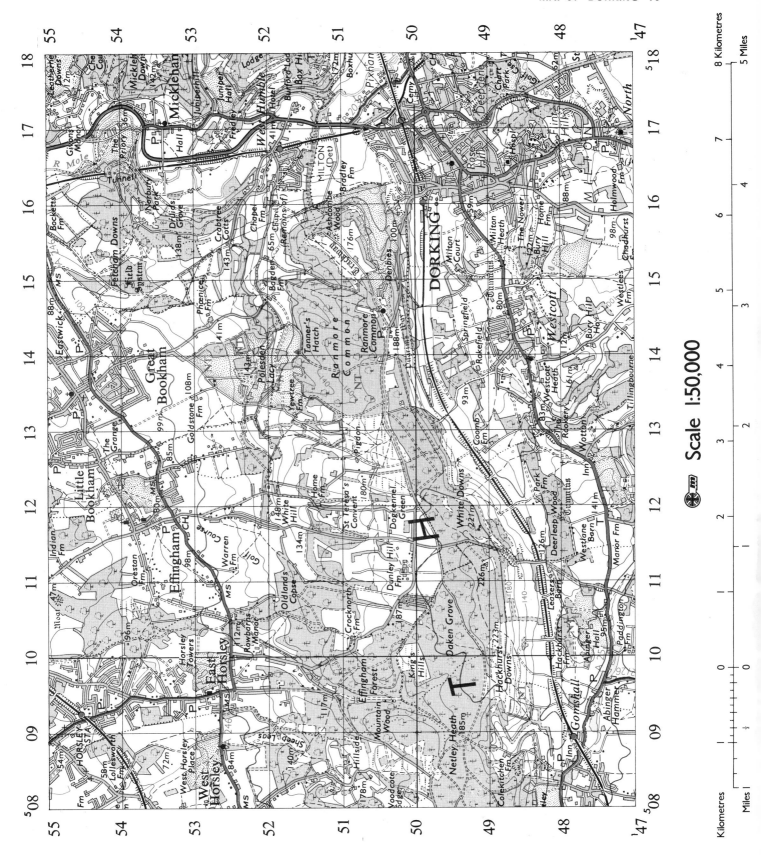

Scale 1:50,000

Reproduced from the Ordnance Survey Map with the sanction of The Controller of H.M. Stationery Office. Crown Copyright reserved.

Chapter Sixteen: Metric Maps: Dorking Map 9

This map has been drawn to the decimal scale of 1 : 50,000 and has metric contours with an interval of 20 metres. It has been produced by the Ordnance Survey from a direct photographic enlargement of the one inch map 7th Series, with all heights converted into metric values. It is not part of any existing series of Ordnance Survey maps but it seems likely that when the Ordnance Survey decide their policy on the replacement of the one inch by a metric alternative they will choose this scale and probably this contour interval. We have seen (P. 3) that the scale is 26.72 per cent larger than the 1 : 63,360 map and that consequently the grid squares are longer and the detail clearer than on the former scale. The 20 metre interval is equivalent to 65.616 feet and it is, therefore, somewhat larger than the 50 foot interval on the one inch map. Note that all spot heights are given in metres together with the letter m: The symbol in the margin is that adopted by the British Standards Institute for metrication to bring to the map user's attention that this is a new metric map.

The extract shows part of the North Downs to the west of the Mole Gap at Dorking, part of the Vale of Holmesdale and a little of the country to the south of it. The well known and much used field study centre, Juniper Hall, is located on the eastern margin at Grid Reference 174523, south of Mickleham.

Relief

There are three principal relief divisions: the Downs forming here a marked escarpment and plateau rising to 226 metres which extends south west to north east; the valley of the River Mole; and the narrow vale at the foot of the scarp slope. This slope which faces south has a relief of the order of 100 metres. The back slope falls away to the north and is much dissected by small steep-sided valleys which generally decline northwards except the well marked valleys which lead to the Mole valley from Polesden Lacy and Juniper Hall. The highest parts of the plateau and scarp face are well wooded with mixed conifers and deciduous trees on Netley Heath and Ranmore Common.

Drainage

Apart from the River Mole and the small streams in the southern part of the map which drain east and west from a low watershed there is a marked absence of surface drainage and many dry valleys. Note particularly the example cut into the scarp face in Grid Square 0948. The River Mole swings across its valley between steep river cliffs and has built a flat floodplain first on one side and then on the other. This evidence therefore suggests a highly permeable upland plateau with impermeable alluvium in the Mole valley and other impermeable rocks in the vale to the south. The actual rock outcrops and the main relief features are shown in the geological cross section, Figure 40, shown along grid line Easting 118. Note the flat-topped nature of the chalk crest and the occurrence of a thin deposit of clay-with-flints which coincides with the wooded areas. Compare this part of the North Downs with the chalk escarpment of the South Downs illustrated in Figure 24.

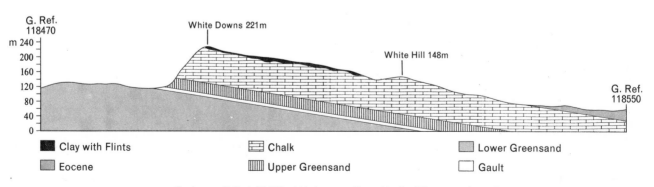

FIG. 40 Geological section across North Downs.

Settlement and Communications

The Pilgrim's Way and other ancient trackways can be traced along the higher ground but the main roads follow the Vale of Holmesdale and the lower part of the back slope in the north and the Mole valley. Here, too, are the main line railways. The narrowing of the Mole gap in the north has restricted the course of the road and the railway has been tunnelled through a pronounced spur.

This area lies about 35 kilometres south west of London and within the commuter belt of daily travel to and from the city, so that most of the villages and Dorking itself show signs of recent development around the old settlement cores. Examine the lay-out of the villages nearest to London from West Horsley to Great Bookham. But there is evidence too of open spaces, land and large estates preserved by the National Trust, and the opportunity to ramble through this part of London's countryside.

Questions-Map 9

1. State the distance in kilometres to the nearest 100 metres along the main road in the north west of the map.

2. Now measure the same distance in inches and using the Representative Fraction only, calculate the distance in miles and furlongs.

3. Calculate the average gradient of the secondary road from its junction at 114497 to the southern end of the quarry at 112486.

4. Draw an annotated sketch map at a scale of 1 : 25,000 to show the relief features of the Mole valley north of Dorking.

5. Why are some of the National Trust properties shown in red and others in blue?

6. If this area were invaded by the sea to a height of 200 metres which points of the map would remain as dry land?

Chapter Seventeen: Metric Maps: Exmouth Map 10

The imprint of the British Standards Institute sign in the margin shows that this map extract is not in the normal 1 : 25,000 series published by the Ordnance Survey. This scale has gained an increasing popularity since it was first published shortly after the end of the second world war and maps are now issued in the second Regular Edition for some parts of the United Kingdom. A whole sheet measures 10 by 20 kilometres instead of 10 by 10 kilometres in the provisional and First Regular editions and also differs from the latter in the strength of the colour used to show contours and roads and in the addition of green to depict woodland and rights of way. But the special feature of this map which makes it a fully metric example is that all height is given in metres with contours at 5 metre intervals.

The map shows part of the coast of east Devon at the mouth of the river Exe and around the coastal resort of Exmouth. To the north the roads lead to the city of Exeter and to the east the immediate rail link is with Budleigh Salterton.

Questions-Map 10

1. Construct a cross section north to south along grid line easting 03 to show relief. Use a vertical interval of 2 millimetres to 5 metres.

2. Reduce the scale to 1 : 50,000 and draw a sketch map showing: the outline of the coast, the Littleham and Withycombe Brooks, all land above 100 metres, a dry valley. Add a scale of Kilometres.

3. Prepare a sketch map on a scale of 1 : 10,000 of the features south of grid line northing 80.

4. Using tracing paper and the squares method estimate the area in square kilometres of woodland drawn on the map.

5. Describe a walk along the coastal footpath starting at—Grid Reference 013799.

6. What evidence is there on the map that Exmouth is primarily a holiday and residential centre?

7. Describe any form of land use shown on the map.

8. Describe what you would see looking due north from West Down Beacon at 129 metres in Grid Square 0481. If necessary construct a sketch and intervisibility section.

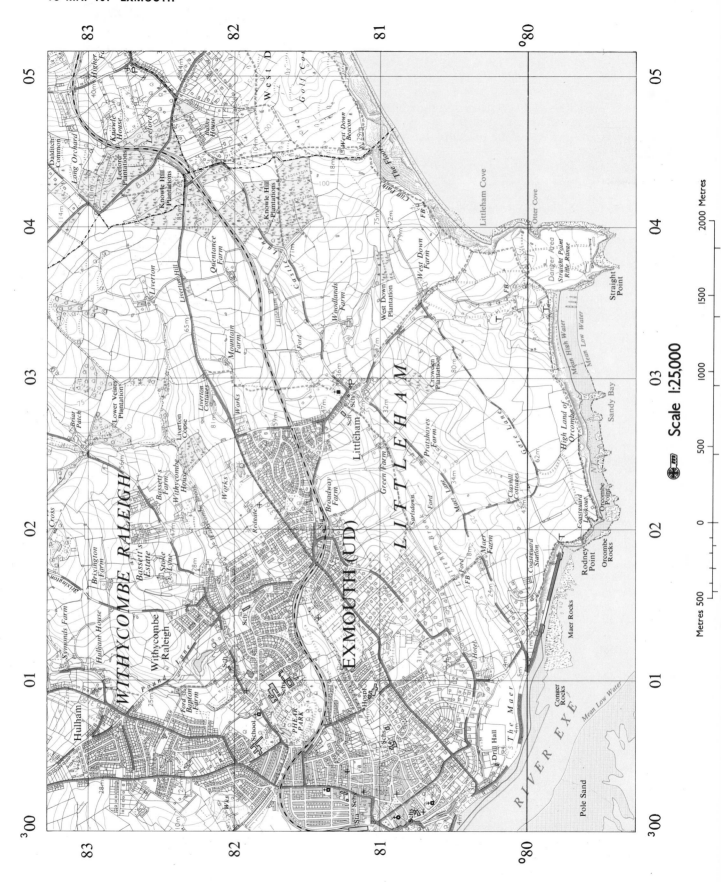

Scale 1:25,000

Reproduced from the Ordnance Survey Map with the sanction of The Controller of H.M. Stationery Office.   Crown Copyright reserved.